The Dome of Heaven

The Dome of Heaven

A Prayer Course for Advent

Lavinia Byrne IBVM

Hodder & Stoughton
LONDON SYDNEY AUCKLAND

Scripture quotations are from the New Revised Standard Version
Bible, Anglicised Edition, copyright © 1989, 1995. Division of
Christian Education of the National Council of the Churches of
Christ in the USA. All rights reserved.

First published in Great Britain in 1999

10 9 8 7 6 5 4 3 2 1

British Library Cataloguing in Publication Data
A record for this book is available from the British Library

ISBN 0 340 72239 8

Typeset by Avon Dataset Ltd, Bidford-on-Avon, Warks.

Printed and bound in Great Britain by
The Guernsey Press Co. Ltd, Channel Isles

Hodder and Stoughton Ltd
A Division of Hodder Headline PLC
338 Euston Road
London NW1 3BH

O God, who made the dome of heaven
And set the stars in place,
Whose sun and moon mark out our days
Creating time and space.

Beloved Father, Lord of all,
Sin drove us from your care
Entrancing us with shows of light:
Deceit, distrust, despair.

Eternal Son, born once in time,
Two thousand years ago;
Restorer of our hope and grace,
From you all mercies flow.

Spirit of glory, source of joy,
Help us to offer praise
And hope-filled prayers and songs and hymns
Through all our future days.

All powerful Trinity of love
Our destiny and home;
Inspire in us a living faith
And call us to your throne.

L.M.B.

To be sung to 'St Anne'

Contents

Introduction

Advent is a time of preparation. It is a holy, a sacred season. For four weeks the Church asks us to make the way straight for the coming of the Messiah. We are called to stand under the judgment of God and, with renewed fervour, to experience his mercy. How can we do this creatively at the turn of a new century and a new millennium?

The Dome of Heaven

A special book for a special Advent, *The Dome of Heaven* provides a wealth of material to reflect on at this time. It offers an alternative vision of what our celebrations can mean. It matches rich texts from the Christian tradition to the anxieties of our own times, showing how the work of God is renewed and strengthened with the passing years. These texts come from sources as varied as the Early Church Fathers and the medieval mystics, the great divines and modern figures, such as Dorothy L. Sayers. So we read what Irenaeus and Augustine, Julian of Norwich and Walter Hilton, John Wesley and Charles Spurgeon have to say to our times. In each and every age, the message of the Gospel has given security and wisdom. It continues to do so. The readings, reflections, prayers and, above all, the exercises take us deep into the meaning of Advent, of Christmas, the Epiphany and of the years to come. This book is intended equally for group or family use and for individuals to enjoy as they renew their life of faith.

Why this title?

> Let us, with a gladsome mind,
> praise the Lord, for he is kind:
> *For his mercies ay endure,*
> *ever faithful, ever sure.*
>
> Let us blaze his name abroad,
> for of gods he is the God:
>
> He with all-commanding might
> filled the new-made world with light:
>
> He the golden-tressèd sun
> caused all day his course to run:
>
> And the hornèd moon by night,
> mid her spangled sisters bright:
>
> All things living he doth feed,
> his full hand supplies their need:
>
> Let us, with a gladsome mind,
> praise the Lord for he is kind:
> *For his mercies ay endure,*
> *ever faithful, ever sure.*

John Milton, 1608–74

Milton's poem reminds us how intense human fascination with the sky has always been. We try to emulate it by creating our own domes, but nothing can match the magnificence of the panoply that nature already holds over us. It reminds us of God's constant care of us and of the tender love within which our world is held in being. We are the first generation to have seen the world from space. Our own mental worlds are constellated differently as a result. We see our planet suspended like a delicate blue and green marble with unimaginable and unfathomable space circling it. We see it spinning in and out of dark and light. Our life on earth is mirrored and echoed to the farthest bounds of recorded time and space, as we discover how our universe was poised from its earliest moments to bring forth the elements of our creation.

We know about the light, as it is where most of us do our most intense living. We crave the 'golden-tressèd sun', especially during winter, and long for its warmth and comfort. But what about the dark? How able are we to stand and stare at the stars and to allow them to shine on us? This Advent is a winter, a seasonal feast. We take time to look at the heavens when we think about the 'hornèd moon by night, mid her spangled sisters bright'. When we look into the dome of heaven, God's dome, we see it in its night-time brilliance as well as during the day.

Why this pattern?

We are invited to become seasonal people, people who inhabit time and space with a sense of its liturgical significance. When we celebrate the coming of God at the darkest season of life in our hemisphere, we realise that we are here to reflect about something sacred and mysterious too. How are we to do this? How can a discipline of prayer during Advent and on through Christmas to the feast of the Epiphany, how can such a discipline help us? We are called to honour God and our own spiritual identity. We are offered resources to meet our need to be in relationship with God. This book is one of them. It is divided into six sections. Because this is a liturgical season, we turn to the liturgy to give us a sense of shape and purpose at this time.

The greatest of all Christian celebrations is the Eucharist. Through our great thanksgiving we offer God praise day by day, Sunday by Sunday. That is why this book has adopted the same pattern as our eucharistic celebrations. We begin with a greeting, an opportunity to stand before God and find ourselves greeted and known by name. God recognises us and we acknowledge the divine presence in our lives. This is the way every eucharistic service begins, be it described as mass or as a communion service. Recognition and love go hand in hand. Yet

Advent is also a time of judgment, a time when we are exposed, in all our rawness, to the mercy of God. That is why we open our hearts and say sorry for our own sins, failings and forgetfulness; for our deceit, lies and doubt. Then God turns to us in love and forgives us in the very depths of our being. We are allowed to let go of all that troubles us and to rest in God's love.

Renewed by the words of absolution, we turn to God afresh and listen to the stories of creation, fall, covenant and salvation. We hear passionate and grand stories, those of our redemption as it is told in the Old and New Testaments. We hear a new gospel, one which assures us that we are invited to enjoy the freedom which God offers us. What are we to do when we learn of so much generosity? Offer ourselves in return. This is the moment when, in our eucharistic celebrations, we bring our gifts to the altar. Our Advent discipline also asks us to think about presents. So we prepare the gifts we will bring to the manger at Christmas: our gold, frankincense and myrrh. The heart of our Eucharist or great act of thanksgiving approaches. We get ready for Christmas by coming close to the mystery of God's appearing among us, the incarnation.

We stay with Mary and Joseph as they receive the communion gift of the real presence of Jesus in the baby who lies in the straw at their feet. Our faith, hope and charity are renewed even as we greet the new century. But then our focus changes. We are drawn to join the Magi and to come to Bethlehem with them. We reflect on the presence of wisdom and wise people in our own lives. Then we prepare to leave, to let go of all that keeps us rooted to the spot. We undertake to travel on further, to continue to search the dome of heaven for more evidence of the Morning Star who rises for our salvation amid its fire and majesty and splendour. Jesus was born for our salvation; Jesus died for our salvation. On both occasions a veil was rent. The dome of heaven gaped open, that we should be allowed in.

Week One: Greeting – Penitence – Forgiveness
Sunday 28 November 1999: God Greets Us

> 'To the one who conquers I will also give the morning star.' (Rev. 2:28)

Advent is a time of hope and expectation. We prepare ourselves to celebrate a new millennium and for a renewal of God's gifts of life and a future. We also use this time to look backwards in thanksgiving for all the gifts we have already received from God.

Scriptural Reading

'I am the Alpha and the Omega,' says the Lord God, who is and who was and who is to come, the Almighty. 'It is I, Jesus, who sent my angel to you with this testimony for the churches. I am the root and the descendant of David, the bright morning star.' The Spirit and the bride say, 'Come.' And let everyone who hears say, 'Come.' And let everyone who is thirsty come. Let anyone who wishes take the water of life as a gift. Amen. Come, Lord Jesus! The grace of the Lord Jesus be with all the saints. Amen. (Rev. 1:8; 22:16–17, 20–1)

Reflection

During Advent we think about the incarnation, about the fact that God became man for us in the person of Jesus and sought us out right in the heart of the human condition, in the place where we live and love and sin and suffer and need healing. God loves us where we are and looks for us where we are. God greets us there and calls us by name. We greet God as Father, Son and Holy Spirit. We name the God who creates us, redeems us and makes us holy.

Advent is a time to receive the gifts and graces of God. During this season we think about the first coming of Jesus, the Saviour who knows our name and writes it in the sky as our heavenly inheritance. We think about his birth in Bethlehem, about his own star in the dome of heaven. We recall the crib, the shepherds, the Magi. We think of Joseph and Mary. But we also reflect on his future coming, when he will be revealed to us in glory as the Lord of all the ages, the master of history and of human destiny, the great liberator who wills and desires and craves our freedom. Jesus calls us to live in the light. 'Come, Lord Jesus', we pray, knowing that his advent is our salvation.

Prayers

All-powerful God,
Increase our strength of will for doing good
That Christ may find an eager welcome at his coming
And call us to his side in the kingdom of heaven,
Where he lives and reigns with you and the Holy Spirit,
World without end, Amen.

Roman Missal

Saviour eternal!
Health and life of the world unfailing,
Light everlasting!
And in verity our redemption,
Grieving that the ages of men must perish
Thro' the tempter's subtlety,
Still in heav'n abiding, thou camest earthward
Of thine own great clemency:
Then freely and graciously
Deigning to assume humanity,

To lost ones and perishing,
Gavest thou thy free deliverance,
Filling all the world with joy.
O Christ, our souls and bodies cleanse
By thy perfect sacrifice;
That we as temples pure and bright
Fit for thine abode may be.
By thy former advent justify,
By thy second grant us liberty:
That when in the might of glory
Thou descendest, Judge of all,
We in raiment undefiled,
Bright may shine, and ever follow,
Lord, thy footsteps blest, where'er they lead us.

Advent Sequence, c. 900, tr. M. J. Blacker

Lead, kindly Light, amid the encircling gloom,
    Lead thou me on;
The night is dark, and I am far from home,
    Lead thou me on.
Keep thou my feet; I do not ask to see
The distant scene; one step enough for me.

I was not ever thus, nor prayed that thou
    Should'st lead me on;
I loved to choose and see my path; but now
    Lead thou me on.
I loved the garish day, and, spite of fears,
Pride ruled my will: remember not past years.

So long thy power hath blessed me, sure it still
    Will lead me on.
O'er moor and fen, o'er crag and torrent, till
    The night is gone;
And with the morn those angel faces smile,
Which I have loved long since, and lost awhile.

John Henry Newman, 1801–90

7

Now the virginity of Mary was hidden from the prince of this world, as was also her offspring, and the death of the Lord; three mysteries of renown, which were wrought in silence by God. How, then, was he manifested to the world? A star shone forth in heaven above all the other stars, the light of which was inexpressible, while its novelty struck us with astonishment. And all the rest of the stars, with the sun and moon, formed a chorus to this star, and its light was exceedingly great above them all. And there was agitation felt as to whence this new spectacle came, so unlike to everything else in the heavens. Hence every kind of magic was destroyed, and every bond of wickedness disappeared; ignorance was removed, and the old kingdom abolished, God himself being manifested in human form for the renewal of eternal life. And now that took a beginning which had been prepared by God. Henceforth all things were in a state of tumult, because he meditated the abolition of death. (Ignatius of Antioch, d. 107, *The Epistle to the Ephesians*, 19)

Almighty God, give us grace that we may cast away the works of darkness, and put upon us the armour of light, now in the time of this mortal life, in which thy Son Jesus Christ came to visit us in great humility; that in the last day, when he shall come again in his glorious majesty to judge both the quick and the dead, we may rise to the life immortal, through him who liveth and reigneth with thee and the Holy Ghost, now and for ever, Amen. (Collect for the First Sunday in Advent, *Book of Common Prayer*)

Exercise

Today you begin to prepare yourself spiritually to receive the Christ child in his Advent coming and at Christmas. You prepare for a new century and a new millennium. Today you take a risk, because you reveal your deepest yearnings and desires. You make a concrete investment in the future by undertaking to pray for grace and hope and life. To help yourself, draw a star. Write your name on it. Where would you like to pin this star right now? Where does the future lie for you?

Monday 29 November 1999: *We Greet God*

'O Lord, our Sovereign, how majestic is your name in all the earth!' (Ps. 8:9)

God greets us, we greet God. Every encounter with God is a welcome to us. Here we are known and acknowledged. Here we are recognised. Everything else falls into place. God is our all in all.

Scriptural Reading

O Lord, our Sovereign, how majestic is your name in all the earth! You have set your glory above the heavens. Out of the mouths of babes and infants you have founded a bulwark because of your foes, to silence the enemy and the avenger. When I look at your heavens, the work of your fingers, the moon and the stars that you have established; what are human beings that you are mindful of them, mortals that you care for them? Yet you have made them a little lower than God, and crowned them with glory and honour. You have given them dominion over the works of your hands; you have put all things under their feet, all sheep and oxen, and also the beasts of the field, the birds of the air, and the

9

fish of the sea, whatever passes along the paths of the seas. O Lord, our Sovereign, how majestic is your name in all the earth! (Ps. 8:1–9)

Reflection

God's name is majestic in all the earth. During Advent we are able to think about the grand and the small-scale work of God. On the grand scale we remember the might and majesty of God. We gaze into the dome of heaven and see the sun and the moon and the stars which are established and held in being there. In our own lives too, we see the inalienable bits of experience – some of our choosing, some not. These are clear evidence of the hand of God in making us who and what we are.

Then there is the small-scale activity, the daily work of God in shaping us into being. Some of this activity will seem so slight that we miss catching hold of it. Like dew or mist, God's constant care for us covers and waters and nourishes us.

When God greets us and calls us to an encounter of grace, what are we to do? Let go. Let go of all the reactions we suppose that we are meant to have. Let go of our fear and suspicion and hostility. Let go of our hopes. Let go of anything that gets in the way. God greets us. God knows us and all that troubles us. In this encounter we are safe because we are known by name.

Prayers

Lord, our God,
Help us to prepare
For the coming of Christ your Son.
May he find us waiting,
Eager in joyful prayer.
We ask this through our Lord Jesus Christ, your Son,
who lives and reigns with you and the Holy Spirit,
one God, for ever and ever, Amen.

Roman Missal

He is Lord, because he rules over the universe; Father, because he is before all things; Fashioner and Maker, because he is creator and maker of the universe; the Highest, because of being above all; and Almighty, because he himself rules and embraces all. For the heights of heaven, and the depths of the abysses, and the ends of the earth, are in his hand, and there is no place of his rest. For the heavens are his work, the earth is his creation, the sea is his handiwork; we are his formation and his image; sun, moon, and stars are his elements, made for signs, and seasons, and days, and years, that they may serve and be slaves to us; and all things God has made out of things that were not into things that are, in order that through his works his greatness may be known and understood. (Theophilus of Antioch, second century, *Letter to Autolycus* 1.4)

> Come, thou long-expected Jesus,
> Born to set thy people free;
> From our fears and sins release us;
> Let us find our rest in thee.
>
> Israel's strength and consolation,
> Hope of all the earth thou art;
> Dear desire of every nation,
> Joy of every longing heart.
>
> Born thy people to deliver;
> Born a child, and yet a king;
> Born to reign in us for ever;
> Now thy gracious kingdom bring.
>
> By thine own eternal Spirit
> Rule in all our hearts alone;
> By thine all-sufficient merit
> Raise us to thy glorious throne.
>
> Charles Wesley, 1707–88

We pray you, O God,
Graciously to cleanse our souls
And our consciences,
That as Christ comes to our hearts
He may find them made ready for himself. Amen.

Precamur nostras in *York Missal II*

Exercise

'O Lord, our Sovereign, how majestic is your name in all the earth!' Repeat these words over and over again. Let them get into your bloodstream. Say the first half on an in-breath and the other half as you breathe out. 'O Lord, our Sovereign, how majestic is your name in all the earth!' Repeat this exercise during the day.

Tuesday 30 November 1999: We Name Our Sins

'You desire truth in the inward being; therefore teach me wisdom in my secret heart.' (Ps. 51:6)

God desires truth in our innermost being. God offers us the possibility of honesty, self-disclosure, comfort, forgiveness, peace. When we come into the divine presence, we pray for wisdom in our secret heart. When we face judgment, we meet mercy.

Scriptural Reading

Have mercy on me, O God, according to your steadfast love; according to your abundant mercy blot out my transgressions. Wash me thoroughly from my iniquity,

and cleanse me from my sin. For I know my transgressions, and my sin is ever before me. Against you,
you alone, have I sinned, and done what is evil in your
sight, so that you are justified in your sentence and
blameless when you pass judgment. Create in me a
clean heart, O God, and put a new and right spirit within
me. Do not cast me away from your presence, and do
not take your holy spirit from me. Restore to me the
joy of your salvation, and sustain in me a willing spirit.
Then I will teach transgressors your ways, and sinners
will return to you. (Ps. 51:1–4, 10–13)

Reflection

When we come into the presence of God and start to pray, we
are given an opportunity, an opening. For we are able to be
completely honest about ourselves and our needs. We can tell
God who we are.

This means acknowledging our own wrongdoing. It means
trust. Only when I say that I have done wrong can I ask for
forgiveness. I need to say that I have done wrong. Only when I
am truthful can I receive the gift which God is so constant in
offering me: the grace of acceptance. God's acceptance of us is
utter and total and overwhelming. We are known and loved and
accepted, whatever we have done or failed to do. We are cradled
and sheltered and protected. Our name is held in the dome of
heaven. We are constellated as a fixed point in God's universe.

Prayer is something personal, something we do out of con-
viction. But it is also something bigger than ourselves: it is
part of a dance of the whole of creation. It calls us together
from north, south, east and west. When we pray for forgiveness
we do so for ourselves but also for everyone. Our prayer has
cosmic significance. It takes us right back to the first sin of our
first parents, to the moment when God's intervention became
an absolute requirement in human life. The God who first
created us became our Redeemer. Jesus was born for our
salvation.

Prayers

O thou who through the light of nature hast aroused in us a longing for the light of grace, so that we may be raised in the light of thy majesty, to thee I give thanks, Creator and Lord, that thou allowest me to rejoice in thy works. Praise the Lord ye heavenly harmonies, and ye who know the revealed harmonies. For from him, through him and in him, all is, which is perceptible as well as spiritual; that which we know and that which we do not know, for there is still much to learn. (Johann Kepler, 1571–1630)

If I were but mere dust and ashes I might speak unto the Lord, for the Lord's hand made me of this dust, and the Lord's hand shall re-collect these ashes; the Lord's hand was the wheel upon which this vessel of clay was framed, and the Lord's hand is the urn in which these ashes shall be preserved. I am the dust and the ashes of the temple of the Holy Ghost, and what marble is so precious? But I am more than dust and ashes: I am my best part, I am my soul. And being so, the breath of God, I may breathe back these pious expostulations to my God: My God, my God, why is not my soul as sensible as my body? Why hath not my soul these apprehensions, these presages, these changes, these antidates, these jealousies, these suspicions of a sin, as well as my body of a sickness? Why is there not always a pulse in my soul to beat at the approach of a temptation to sin? Why are there not always waters in mine eyes, to testify my spiritual sickness? I stand in the way of temptations, naturally, necessarily; all men do so; for there is a snake in every path, temptations in every vocation; but I go, I run, I fly into the ways of temptation which I might shun; nay, I break into houses where the plague is, I press into places of temptation, and tempt the devil himself, and solicit and importune

14

them who had rather be left unsolicited by me. I fall sick
of sin, and am bedded and bedrid, buried and putrified
in the practice of sin, and all this while have no presage,
no pulse, no sense of my sickness. (John Donne, 1571–
1631, *Devotions upon Emergent Occasions*)

Hills of the north, rejoice,
    river and mountain-spring,
hark to the advent voice;
    valley and lowland, sing.
Christ comes in righteousness and love,
he brings salvation from above.

Isles of the southern seas,
    sing to the listening earth;
carry on every breeze
    hope of a world's new birth:
in Christ shall all be made anew;
his word is sure, his promise true.

Lands of the East, arise,
    he is your brightest morn,
greet him with joyous eyes,
    praise shall his path adorn:
the God whom you have longed to know
in Christ draws near, and calls you now.

Shores of the utmost west,
    lands of the setting sun,
welcome the heavenly guest
    in whom the dawn has come:
he brings a never-ending light,
who triumphed o'er our darkest night.

Shout, as you journey home;
    songs be in every mouth!
Lo, from the north they come,
    from east and west and south:

in Jesus all shall find their rest,
in him the universe be blest.

Charles E. Oakley, 1832–65

God of mercy and consolation,
Help us in our weakness and free us from sin.
Hear our prayers
That we may rejoice at the coming of your Son,
Who lives and reigns with you and the Holy Spirit,
One God, for ever and ever, Amen.

Roman Missal

Exercise

Write a list of your three most frequent sins. Be as honest as you can be about this. Ask God's forgiveness for them one by one, and experience the full force of divine grace as it speaks to you in your time of need.

Wednesday 1 December 1999: Our World's Sins

'We will all stand before the judgment seat of God.' (Rom. 14:10)

A millennium celebration invites us to look forwards and to plan a new future. It also offers us the chance to repent of the sins of our world, confident that God wills our life and freedom.

Scriptural Reading

Therefore you have no excuse, whoever you are, when you judge others; for in passing judgment on another you condemn yourself, because you, the judge, are doing the very same things. You say, 'We know that God's judgment on those who do such things is in accordance with truth.' Do you imagine, whoever you are, that when you judge those who do such things and yet do them yourself, you will escape the judgment of God? Or do you despise the riches of his kindness and forbearance and patience? Do you not realise that God's kindness is meant to lead you to repentance? But by your hard and impenitent heart you are storing up wrath for yourself on the day of wrath, when God's righteous judgment will be revealed. For he will repay according to each one's deeds: to those who by patiently doing good seek for glory and honour and immortality, he will give eternal life; while for those who are self-seeking and who obey not the truth but wickedness, there will be wrath and fury. (Rom. 2:1–8)

Reflection

'Do you not realise that God's kindness is meant to lead you to repentance?' There is only one reason for reflecting on our sins: God calls us into the light. We are invited to repent and so to receive the full grace of forgiveness. But we do not come to forgiveness on our own, just as we do not commit sins in a lone world where there are no other people and our actions have no consequences for others. We are part of a world which has been shaped by centuries – and now two millennia – of human experience. Some of this experience is bright and glorious: it mirrors and reflects God's desires for us. It represents fidelity to the call of God. Some of it is a shadow history. It shows us how selfish and fearful we have been.

The legacy is a troubling one. For human greed and pride have dominated us and we have fought wars and waged battles in their name. We have hurt each other in mind and body because we are afraid of differences of race or class or colour or gender or sexual orientation. We have developed exploitative economies. We have snatched at resources rather than sharing them with others. We have not been good neighbours. With the coming of the millennium we have the opportunity to take stock: to fine-tune our sense of commitment to other people and to the urgency of their needs. This requires contrition from us. We kneel down and say sorry to God because, despite the intervention of his divine Son, we have failed to take the gospel to our hearts.

Prayers

Lord our God,
Grant that we may be ready
To receive Christ when he comes in glory
And to share in the banquet of heaven,
Where he lives and reigns with you and the Holy Spirit,
One God, for ever and ever, Amen.

Roman Missal

Hark, a thrilling voice is sounding;
'Christ is nigh', it seems to say;
'Cast away the dreams of darkness,
O ye children of the day.'

Wakened by the solemn warning,
Let the earth-bound soul arise;
Christ, her sun, all ill dispelling,
Shines upon the morning skies.

Lo, the Lamb, so long expected,
Comes with pardon down from heaven;
Let us haste with tears of sorrow,
One and all to be forgiven;

That when next he comes with glory,
And the world is wrapped in fear,
With his mercy he may shield us,
And with words of love draw near.

Honour, glory, might, and blessing
To the Father and the Son,
With the everlasting Spirit,
While eternal ages run.
Latin, sixth century, tr. Edward Caswall, 1814–78

God himself, who is almighty, the Creator of all things,
and invisible, has sent from heaven, and placed among
us, him who is the truth, and the holy and incompre-
hensible Word, and has firmly established him in our
hearts. He did not, as one might have imagined, send
to us any servant, or angel, or ruler, or any one of those
who bear sway over earthly things, or one of those to
whom the government of things in the heavens has been
entrusted, but the very Creator and Fashioner of all
things – by whom he made the heavens – by whom he
enclosed the sea within its proper bounds – whose
ordinances all the stars faithfully observe – from whom
the sun has received the measure of his daily course to
be observed – whom the moon obeys, being commanded to shine in the night, and whom the stars also
obey, following the moon in her course; by whom all
things have been arranged, and placed within their
proper limits, and to whom all are subject – the heavens
and the things that are therein, the earth and the things
that are therein, the sea and the things that are therein
– fire, air, and the abyss – the things which are in the
heights, the things which are in the depths, and the
things which lie between. This messenger he sent to
them. Was it then, as one might conceive, for the
purpose of exercising tyranny, or of inspiring fear and
terror? By no means, but under the influence of
clemency and meekness. As a king sends his son, who
is also a king, so sent he him; as God he sent him; as a
Saviour he sent him, and as seeking to persuade, not to
compel us; for violence has no place in the character of

God. As calling us he sent him, not as vengefully pursuing us; as loving us he sent him, not as judging us. (Anon., second century, *The Epistle to Diognetus,* 7)

> Lord God most merciful,
> We confess that we have sinned,
> Through our own fault,
> And in common with others,
> In thought, word, and deed,
> And through what we have left undone.
>
> We ask to be forgiven.
>
> By the power of your Spirit
> Turn us from evil to good,
> Help us to forgive others,
> And keep us in your ways
> Of righteousness and love;
> Through Jesus Christ our Lord, Amen.
>> United Reformed Church, Act of Contrition

O God, who has bound us together in this bundle of life, give us grace to understand how our lives depend on the industry, honesty and integrity of others; that we may be mindful of their needs, grateful for their faithfulness, and faithful in our responsibilities to them; through Jesus Christ our Lord, Amen. (Reinhold Niebuhr, 1892–1971)

Exercise

Watch the TV news bulletin or listen to the news on the radio. Notice what gets reported and what gets ignored. Who is being glamorised and who demonised? Where is the sin? Notice what you feel about this.

Thursday 2 December 1999:
Jesus Saves Us

'In him we have redemption through his blood, the forgiveness of our trespasses.' (Eph. 1:7)

When we acknowledge our sins and wrongdoing, we face a choice. At the beginning of every liturgical service – just as at the beginning of Advent – we are offered absolution. This is our choice today. Can we turn to God for forgiveness or not?

Scriptural Reading
Blessed be the God and Father of our Lord Jesus Christ, who has blessed us in Christ with every spiritual blessing in the heavenly places, just as he chose us in Christ before the foundation of the world to be holy and blameless before him in love. He destined us for adoption as his children through Jesus Christ, according to the good pleasure of his will, to the praise of his glorious grace that he freely bestowed on us in the Beloved. In him we have redemption through his blood, the forgiveness of our trespasses, according to the riches of his grace that he lavished on us. With all wisdom and insight he has made known to us the mystery of his will, according to his good pleasure that he set forth in Christ, as a plan for the fullness of time, to gather up all things in him, things in heaven and things on earth. (Eph. 1:3–10)

Reflection
At Christmas, we celebrate a birth, that of Jesus, who was born for our salvation. He forgives us our personal sins; he forgives

21

the sins of our world and of our age. Jesus is our Redeemer. This means that we can enter and stand in the presence of God with hope and courage. We can take our place where we belong – in the glory of the saints.

But when we sin, or when we experience depression or sadness, the glory of the saints feels a long way away from where we are. When we are traumatised, God feels absent. Yet Jesus comes to us, Jesus approaches us. He calls us by name. Hear him now calling your name. Hear the gentle tone of his voice. Forget all the harsh or forbidding voices you have heard – even those which seem to come from the Church. The only forgiving voice is that which you hear from your Lord and Saviour, from the Lord who loves you into life and wills your freedom. Trust in him. He is your Saviour; he is your Redeemer. No one else can save you.

The work of the incarnation and of the cross belong together. Jesus was born for our salvation.

Prayers

Thanks be to thee, O Lord Jesus Christ, for all the benefits which thou hast given us; for all the pains and insults which thou hast borne for us. O most merciful Redeemer, friend and brother, may we know thee more clearly, love thee more dearly, and follow thee more nearly; for thine own sake. Amen.

The Prayer of Richard of Chichester

Creator of the stars of night,
Thy people's everlasting light,
Jesus, Redeemer, save us all,
And hear thy servants when they call.

Thou, grieving that the ancient curse
Should doom to death a universe,
Hast found the medicine, full of grace,
To save and heal a ruined race.

Thou camest Bridegroom of the bride,
As drew the world to evening-tide;
Proceeding from a virgin shrine,
The spotless Victim all divine:

At whose dread name, majestic now,
All knees in heaven and earth must bow;
And things celestial thee shall own,
And things terrestrial, Lord alone.

O thou whose coming is with dread
To judge and doom the quick and dead,
Preserve us, while we dwell below,
From every insult of the foe.

To God the Father, God the Son,
And God the Spirit, Three in One,
Laud, honour, might, and glory be
From age to age eternally. Amen.

Conditur alme siderum, seventh century, tr. J. M. Neale

Father,
We need your help.
Free us from sin and bring us to life.
Support us by your power.
Grant this through our Lord Jesus Christ, your Son,
Who lives and reigns with you and the Holy Spirit,
One God, for ever and ever, Amen.

Roman Missal

None else, now, is found in the Scriptures but the common Saviour of all, the Word of God, our Lord Jesus Christ. For he it is that proceeded from a virgin and appeared as man on the earth, and whose generation after the flesh cannot be declared. For there is none that can tell his father after the flesh, his body not being of a man, but of a virgin alone; so that no one can declare the corporal generation of the Saviour from a man, in the same way as one can draw up a genealogy of David and of Moses and of all the patriarchs. For he it is that caused the star also to mark the birth of his body; since it was fit that the Word, coming down from heaven, should have his constellation also from heaven, and it was fitting that the King of Creation when he came forth should be openly recognised by all creation. (Athanasius, 296–373, *On the Incarnation of the Word*, 37)

Exercise

Jesus is our Saviour. We are redeemed, forgiven. Say the prayer of Richard of Chichester over and over again. 'O most merciful redeemer, friend and brother, may we know thee more clearly, love thee more dearly, and follow thee more nearly; for thine own sake. Amen.'

Friday 3 December 1999: We Receive Forgiveness

'We even boast in God through our Lord Jesus Christ, through whom we have now received reconciliation.' (Rom. 5:11)

We hear consoling words as we open our hearts to the work of redemptive love. 'May Almighty God have mercy on us, forgive us our sins and bring us to everlasting life, Amen.'

Scriptural Reading

For while we were still weak, at the right time Christ died for the ungodly. Indeed, rarely will anyone die for a righteous person – though perhaps for a good person someone might actually dare to die. But God proves his love for us in that while we still were sinners Christ died for us. Much more surely then, now that we have been justified by his blood, will we be saved through him from the wrath of God. For if while we were enemies, we were reconciled to God through the death of his Son, much more surely, having been reconciled, will we be saved by his life. But more than that, we even boast in God through our Lord Jesus Christ, through whom we have now received reconciliation. (Rom. 5:6–11)

Reflection

We receive forgiveness from God. We take it into ourselves and live the life of the reconciled, secure in the knowledge that we are held in love. This is only possible because of the redeeming work of Jesus. During Advent, we are given the opportunity to reflect on the fact that, right from the moment of his conception, Jesus was our Messiah, or Saviour. The promise of forgiveness was kept by him for us.

So how are we to live as forgiven people? What is required of us is faith, which means having a loving and trusting relationship with God who is Father, Son and Holy Spirit. We think about the events of two thousand years ago; about the journey to Bethlehem which Mary began to make. We think about the Father sending Jesus forth into the world, about the Spirit which hovered over the waters at the first creation and now hovers over Mary. We think about the incarnate Son of God in this human baby. And as we reflect on them, we cast our minds forward to nowadays and to our own need for God, praying for a sense of mission for ourselves, for a sense of the Spirit's activity in our lives and for contact with Jesus in our own humanity.

Prayers
Jesus, our Lord
Save us from our sins.
Come, protect us from all dangers
And lead us to salvation,
For you live and reign with the Father and the Holy Spirit,
One God, for ever and ever, Amen.

Roman Missal

Hark the glad sound! The Saviour comes,
   The Saviour promised long!
Let every heart prepare a throne,
   And every voice a song.

He comes the prisoners to release
   In Satan's bondage held;
The gates of brass before him burst,
   The iron fetters yield.

He comes the broken heart to bind,
   The bleeding soul to cure,
And with the treasures of his grace
   To enrich the humble poor.

Our glad hosannas, Prince of peace,
   Thy welcome shall proclaim,
And heaven's eternal arches ring
   With thy beloved name.

Philip Doddridge, 1702–51

We are told by those who have studied the subject, that those gleams which follow each other so fast through the air at night and which some call shooting stars, are nothing but the air itself streaming into the upper regions of the sky under stress of some particular blasts. They say that the fiery track is traced along the sky when those blasts ignite in the ether. In like manner, then, as this air round the earth is forced upwards by some blast and changes into the pure splendour of the ether, so the human mind leaves this murky miry world, and under the stress of the spirit becomes pure and luminous in contact with the true and supernal purity; in such an atmosphere it even itself emits light, and is so filled with radiance, that it becomes itself a light, according to the promise of our Lord that 'the righteous should shine forth as the sun.' We see this even here, in the case of a mirror, or a sheet of water, or any smooth surface that can reflect the light; when they receive the sunbeam they beam themselves; but they would not do this if any stain marred their pure and shining surface. We shall become then as the light, in our nearness to Christ's true light, if we leave this dark atmosphere of the earth and dwell above; and we shall be light, as our Lord says somewhere to his disciples, if the true light that shineth in the dark comes down even to us; unless, that is, any foulness of sin spreading over our hearts should dim the brightness of our light. Perhaps these examples have led us gradually on to the discovery that we can be changed into something better than ourselves; and it has been proved as well that this union of the soul with the incorruptible Deity can be accomplished in no other way but by herself attaining by her virgin state to the utmost purity possible, – a state which, being like God, will enable her to grasp that to which it is like, while she places herself like a mirror beneath the purity of God, and molds her own beauty at the touch and the sight of the Archetype of all beauty. (Gregory of Nyssa, 330–95, *On Virginity,* 11)

Exercise
Look carefully in a mirror and notice the evidence of your own humanity. Offer it up to God, praying to be moulded and sculpted in the image of the Archetype of all beauty.

Saturday 4 December 1999: We Rest in God's Love

'Rejoice with me, for I have found my sheep that was lost.' (Luke 15:6)

Today we reflect on the joy God experiences when sinners repent. We rest in the sense that God knows and loves us.

Scriptural Reading

So Jesus told them this parable: 'Which one of you, having a hundred sheep and losing one of them, does not leave the ninety-nine in the wilderness and go after the one that is lost until he finds it? When he has found it, he lays it on his shoulders and rejoices. And when he comes home, he calls together his friends and neighbours, saying to them, "Rejoice with me, for I have found my sheep that was lost." Just so, I tell you, there will be more joy in heaven over one sinner who repents than over ninety-nine righteous persons who need no repentance.

'Or what woman having ten silver coins, if she loses one of them, does not light a lamp, sweep the house, and search carefully until she finds it?' (Luke 15:3–8)

Reflection

Two powerful images to depict the care God takes to search us out and restore us to our true identity when we have strayed. Two stories which remind us how precious we are. But above all, two snapshots of the mood and feelings which Jesus attributes to God. Here we see a God who rejoices at the recovery of what was lost and is now found. There is happiness in heaven when a sinner turns to God and asks for pardon and forgiveness. Nothing has to be negotiated; nothing has to be bargained over. All is gift. All is grace.

Each of the items which are lost is part of a greater whole. One sheep goes missing; the ninety-nine are safe. One coin rolls away; the other nine are in a jam jar or an old sock. We are never alone in what we do before God but rather we belong together as part of a greater whole. Forgiveness from God restores us to communion and to community. We are free to be ourselves because relationship is restored to us and we pick up the thread of our friendships again, once we live in an ordered way. The right ordering of our relationships mirrors the joy God experiences at finding us.

Prayers

God our Father,
You loved the world so much
You gave your only Son to free us
From the ancient power of sin and death.
Help us who wait for his coming,
And lead us to true liberty.
We ask this through our Lord Jesus Christ, your Son,
Who lives and reigns with you and the Holy Spirit,
One God, for ever and ever, Amen.

Roman Missal

Lo! He comes with clouds descending,
　　Once for favoured sinners slain;
Thousand thousand Saints attending
　　Swell the triumph of his train:
　　　　Alleluya!
　　God appears, on earth to reign.

Every eye shall now behold him
　　Robed in dreadful majesty;
Those who set at nought and sold him,

29

Pierced and nailed him to the tree,
　　Deeply wailing
　Shall the true Messiah see.

Those dear tokens of his passion
　Still his dazzling body bears,
Cause of endless exultation
　To his ransomed worshippers:
　　With what rapture
　Gaze we on those glorious scars!

Yea, amen! Let all adore thee,
　High on thine eternal throne;
Saviour, take the power and glory:
　Claim the kingdom for thine own:
　　O come quickly!
　Alleluya! Come, Lord, come!

　　　　　　　　　Charles Wesley, 1707–88

We have been bought with too great a price for our Redeemer to let us slip. Therefore, let us march on with confidence, hearing our Redeemer say to us, 'When thou passest through the waters, I will be with thee; and through the rivers, they shall not overflow thee: when thou walkest through the fire, thou shalt not be burned; neither shall the flame kindle upon thee.' Concerning his redeemed, the Lord will say to the enemy, 'Touch not mine anointed, and do my prophets no harm.' The stars in their courses fight for the ransomed of the Lord. If their eyes were opened, they would see the mountain full of horses of fire and chariots of fire round about them. Oh, how my weary heart prizes redeeming love! If it were not for this, I would lay me down, and die. Friends forsake me, foes surround me, I am filled with contempt, and tortured with the subtlety which I cannot baffle; but as the Lord of all brought again from the dead our Lord Jesus, that

great Shepherd of the sheep, by the blood of the everlasting covenant, so by the blood of his covenant doth
he loose his prisoners, and sustain the hearts of those
who tremble at his Word. 'O my soul, thou hast trodden
down strength,' for the Lord hath said unto thee, 'Fear
not: for I have redeemed thee.' (Charles H. Spurgeon,
1834–92, *Till He Come: Communion Meditations and
Addresses*)

Exercise
Listen to a piece of music that makes you really happy and
imagine the joy of God at your redemption and reconciliation
to communion with the company of the saints on earth and in
heaven.

Week Two: God's Story, Our Story
Sunday 5 December 1999:
Creation

'And God saw that it was good.' (Gen. 1:10)

We begin to listen to the great stories of how God made and saved us. Today we hear how God made the world and all that it contains.

Scriptural Reading

O Lord, how manifold are your works! In wisdom you have made them all; the earth is full of your creatures. Yonder is the sea, great and wide, creeping things innumerable are there, living things both small and great. There go the ships, and Leviathan that you formed to sport in it. These all look to you to give them their food in due season; when you give to them, they gather it up; when you open your hand, they are filled with good things. When you hide your face, they are dismayed; when you take away their breath, they die and return to their dust. When you send forth your spirit, they are created; and you renew the face of the ground. May the glory of the Lord endure for ever; may the Lord rejoice in his works – who looks on the earth and it trembles, who touches the mountains and they smoke. I will sing to the Lord as long as I live; I will sing praise to my God while I have being. May my meditation be pleasing to him, for I rejoice in the Lord. (Ps. 104:24–34)

Reflection

This week we listen to the story of the great and central mysteries of our faith. Today is the turn of creation, the story of how we came into being. We reflect on the fact that God is our creator. God made us, fashioned us into being. We get in touch with our own creativity and realise how this confirms our sense that we are made in the divine image and likeness. But there is an added dimension to our understanding of this mystery. When we say that God is our creator, we are not simply talking about the origins of our planet and our universe. Rather we are contemplating the activity of God in our lives now. For today – as every day – we are held in being through the power of the Almighty who breathes us newly into being. So God the creator is also God the sustainer and the nurturer. We are given food in due season, that is to say, all the time. Every day offers us a new start.

Our response to the sheer goodness and magnificence of creation is to sing to the Lord, to offer praise and thanksgiving for the glory of God which is shown to us through created reality. Our response to the amazing fact of our own creation and re-creation is to live as fully and creatively as possible, so that we too exist for the glory and praise of God.

Prayers

Blessed Lord,
   who caused all holy Scriptures
to be written for our learning:
help us so to hear them,
to read, mark, learn, and inwardly digest them
that, through patience, and the comfort
   of your holy word,
we may embrace and for ever hold fast
   the hope of everlasting life,
which you have given us in our Saviour Jesus Christ, Amen.

Collect for Advent 2,
Alternative Service Book 1980

The Dome of Heaven

Let us even dare to own we believe there is a God; nay, and not a lazy, indolent, epicurean deity, who sits at ease upon the circle of the heavens, and neither knows nor cares what is done below; but one who, as he created heaven and earth, and all the armies of them, as he sustains them all by the word of his power, so cannot neglect the work of his own hands. With pleasure we own there is such a God, whose eye pervades the whole sphere of created beings, who knoweth the number of the stars, and calleth them all by their names; a God whose wisdom is as the great abyss, deep and wide as eternity; who, high in power, in the beginning said, Let sea, and air, and earth, and heaven be made: And it was so. Yet more; whose mercy riseth above the heavens, and his faithfulness above the clouds; who is loving to every man, and his mercy over all his works. Let us secure him on our side; let us make this wise, this powerful, this gracious God our friend. Then need we not fear, though the earth be moved, and the hills be carried into the midst of the sea; no, not though the heavens being on fire are dissolved, and the very elements melt with fervent heat. It is enough that the Lord of hosts is with us, the God of love is our everlasting refuge. (John Wesley, 1703–91, *Serious Thoughts occasioned by the Late Earthquake at Lisbon, 1755*)

> The spacious firmament on high,
> With all the blue ethereal sky,
> And spangled heavens, a shining frame,
> Their great original proclaim.
> The unwearied sun from day to day
> Does his Creator's power display,
> And publishes to every land
> The works of an almighty hand.

Soon as the evening shades prevail
The moon takes up the wondrous tale,
And nightly to the listening earth
Repeats the story of her birth;
Whilst all the stars that round her burn,
And all the planets in their turn,
Confirm the tidings, as they roll,
And spread the truth from pole to pole.

What though in solemn silence all
Move round the dark terrestrial ball;
What though nor real voice nor sound
Amid their radiant orbs be found;
In reason's ear they all rejoice,
And utter forth a glorious voice;
For ever singing as they shine,
'The hand that made us is Divine.'

Joseph Addison, 1672–1719

God of power and mercy,
Open our hearts in welcome.
Remove the things that hinder us from receiving
    Christ with joy,
So that we may share his wisdom
And become one with him
When he comes in glory,
For he lives and reigns with you and the Holy Spirit,
One God, for ever and ever, Amen.

Collect for the Second Sunday of Advent,
Roman Missal

Exercise
Make something today: a loaf of bread, a poem, a cup of tea, a list, a flower arrangement. Do something which puts you in touch with your own ability to create. Concentrate on what you are doing and thank God for it.

Monday 6 December 1999:
The Fall

'What is this that you have done?' (Gen. 3:13)

God's question is a challenge to us. It resonates down the ages and picks up echoes in our own lives. But first of all, it was addressed to Eve, after she and Adam had eaten forbidden fruit.

Scriptural Reading

They heard the sound of the Lord God walking in the garden at the time of the evening breeze, and the man and his wife hid themselves from the presence of the Lord God among the trees of the garden. But the Lord God called to the man, and said to him, 'Where are you?' He said, 'I heard the sound of you in the garden, and I was afraid, because I was naked; and I hid myself.' He said, 'Who told you that you were naked? Have you eaten from the tree of which I commanded you not to eat?' The man said, 'The woman whom you gave to be with me, she gave me fruit from the tree, and I ate.' Then the Lord God said to the woman, 'What is this that you have done?' The woman said, 'The serpent tricked me, and I ate.' (Gen. 3:8–13)

Reflection

This is a story about our need for redemption. Because of the act of disobedience of our first parents, Jesus was born for our salvation. This is why some of the earliest of texts refer to the momentous event in the Garden of Eden as a 'happy fault', because it would merit so great a Redeemer. So who are the characters in this drama? Are they so unlike us that we cannot

identify with them, primitive beings in some kind of imaginary
paradise? Or does the story carry a huge human myth for us,
and so have resonances which creep into our unconscious and
haunt us with their double message of betrayal and rejection?

None of us feels worthy to sustain a relationship with God;
we all know about our own betrayals. But what this story visits
and latches into is our sense of rejection. The fact that we can
so easily feel abandoned and cast out by the people we most
love, the fact that we mind so terribly when we lose them –
whether in death, or because they chose other relationships –
the fact of divorce and the breakdown of family life, all of
these feelings are a trigger to our innate sense of fear. The Bible
attributes this fear to a story about rejection from paradise. It
says that these feelings are not unreasonable. But it does more
than that: it offers us redemption. Put simply, it says that our
root relationship – that we have with God – has been regained
for us by Jesus. It is safe, it is secure. We are offered freedom
from fear. The Holy Spirit of God brings us peace. We are to
regain our sense of security, our faith in our own self-worth as
the beloved of God.

Prayers
Lord,
Free us from our sins and make us whole.
Hear our prayer,
And prepare us to celebrate the incarnation of your Son,
Who lives and reigns with you and the Holy Spirit,
One God, for ever and ever, Amen.

Roman Missal

Adam lay ybounden
Bounden in a bond
Four thousand winter
Thought he not too long.

And all was for an apple,
An apple that he took,
As clerkès finden
Written in their book.

Ne had the apple taken been,
The apple taken been,
Ne had never Our Lady
A-been heavenes Queen.

Blessed be the time
That apple taken was.
Therefore we moun singen
Deo gratias!

Medieval carol

The tree of knowledge itself was good, and its fruit
was good. For it was not the tree, as some think, but
the disobedience, which had death in it. And God
showed great kindness to man in this, that he did not
suffer him to remain in sin for ever; but, as it were,
by a kind of banishment, cast him out of Paradise, in
order that, having by punishment expiated, within an
appointed time, the sin, and having been disciplined,
he should afterwards be restored. Wherefore also, when
man had been formed in this world, it is mystically
written in Genesis, as if he had been twice placed in
Paradise; so that the one was fulfilled when he was
placed there, and the second will be fulfilled after the
resurrection and judgment. For just as a vessel, when
on being fashioned it has some flaw, is remoulded or
remade, that it may become new and entire; so also it
happens to man by death. For somehow or other he is
broken up, that he may rise in the resurrection whole;
I mean spotless, and righteous, and immortal. And as
to God's calling, and saying, Where art thou, Adam?
God did this, not as if ignorant of this; but, being long-

suffering, he gave him an opportunity of repentance and confession. (Theophilus of Antioch, second century, *Letter to Autolycus,* 2.28)

O merciful God, the Father of our Lord Jesus Christ, who is the resurrection and the life; in whom whosoever believeth shall live, though he die; and whoever liveth and believeth in him, shall not die eternally; we meekly beseech thee, O Father, to raise us from the death of sin unto the life of righteousness; that when we shall leave this life, we may be found acceptable in thy sight, and receive that blessing which thy well-beloved Son shall pronounce to all that love and fear thee, saying, 'Come ye blessed children of my Father, receive the kingdom prepared for you from the beginning of the world.' Grant this, we beseech thee, O merciful Father, through Jesus Christ, our Mediator and Redeemer. Amen. (Methodist Church, *Book of Offices*)

Exercise

Think of a time when you felt very lost and very abandoned. Try to remember what helped you regain a sense of self-worth. Offer your feelings to God and pray to be renewed by the Holy Spirit. Ask for the friendship of Mary as she continues her journey to Bethlehem. Ask her what it feels like to carry the Saviour of the world.

Tuesday 7 December 1999:
God Offers a Covenant

'I have set my bow in the clouds.' (Gen. 9:13)

The story of the Fall, or of basic insecurity right at the root of our relationship with God, is also a strong theme in the narrative of the Flood. Yet Noah and his family and the animals were saved. We too will be saved. The rainbow, or bow in the clouds, is a blessing and a promise.

Scriptural Reading

Then God said to Noah and to his sons with him, 'As for me, I am establishing my covenant with you and your descendants after you, and with every living creature that is with you, the birds, the domestic animals, and every animal of the earth with you, as many as came out of the ark. I establish my covenant with you, that never again shall all flesh be cut off by the waters of a flood, and never again shall there be a flood to destroy the earth.' God said, 'This is the sign of the covenant that I make between me and you and every living creature that is with you, for all future generations: I have set my bow in the clouds, and it shall be a sign of the covenant between me and the earth. When I bring clouds over the earth and the bow is seen in the clouds, I will remember my covenant that is between me and you and every living creature of all flesh; and the waters shall never again become a flood to destroy all flesh. When the bow is in the clouds, I will see it and remember the everlasting covenant between God and every living creature of all flesh that is on the earth.' God said to Noah, 'This is the sign of the covenant that I have established between me and all flesh that is on the earth.' (Gen. 9:8–17)

Reflection

God makes a promise in a watery world, where a wooden boat or ark offers salvation. This is another of the original stories, the stories that tell us about our very beginnings, our absolute origins. These are human stories of immense importance for us. This particular account of the Flood is full of promise, because God is revealed as the One who is committed to our salvation. There is huge security in what is offered here. For not only does God act on behalf of Noah, but also his intervention through the flood, the ark, the bow in the heavens confirm that he will act again.

What is instituted here is a system for us to recognise God by a series of signs in the outer world which remind us forcibly that God is available to us and acting on our behalf in our inner world as well. God does not simply talk about a covenant. He gets on and makes a covenant with us and then confirms its existence with the creation of a rainbow. Now it could be argued that a rainbow is ephemeral. It is only visible when rain and sunlight fall upon us in a certain combination. But that is a detail: whether we see it or not, the bow in the clouds is there for us. For the true value of the rainbow is that it is a universal phenomenon. Like water and bread and wine and the wood of the ark and the wood of the cross, it is unmistakable and an ever-present reality.

Prayers

Almighty God,
Help us to look forward
To the glory of the birth of Christ our Saviour:
His coming is proclaimed joyfully
To the ends of the earth,
For he lives and reigns with you and the Holy Spirit,
One God, for ever and ever, Amen.

Roman Missal

Lord of our life, and God of our salvation,
Star of our night, and hope of every nation,
Hear and receive thy Church's supplication,
Lord God Almighty.

See round thine ark the hungry billows curling;
See how thy foes their banners are unfurling;
Lord, while their darts envenomed they are hurling,
Thou canst preserve us.

Lord, thou canst help when earthly armour faileth,
Lord, thou canst save when deadly sin assaileth;
Christ, o'er thy Church nor death nor hell prevaileth;
Grant us thy peace, Lord.

Grant us thy help till foes are backward driven;
Grant them thy truth, that they may be forgiven;
Grant peace on earth, and after we have striven,
Peace in thy heaven.

> Matthaus Appelles von Lowenstern, 1594–1648,
> paraphrased by Philip Pusey, 1799–1855

God has said in Isaiah to Jerusalem: 'I saved thee in the deluge of Noah.' By this which God said was meant that the mystery of salvation appeared in the deluge. For righteous Noah, along with the other mortals at the deluge, i.e., with his own wife, his three sons and their wives, being eight in number, were a symbol of the eighth day, wherein Christ appeared when he rose from the dead, for ever the first in power. For Christ, being the first-born of every creature, became again the chief of another race regenerated by himself through water, and faith, and wood, containing the mystery of the cross; even as Noah was saved by wood when he rode over the waters with his household. Accordingly, when the prophet says, 'I saved thee in the times of Noah,' as I have already remarked, he addresses the people who

are equally faithful to God, and possess the same signs.
(Justin Martyr, c. 100–165, *The Second Apology*, 138)

> Salvation has come down to us,
> Of grace and pure goodness.
> Works do not avail any more,
> They cannot save;
> Faith looks to Jesus Christ:
> He has done enough for us all,
> He has become the intercessor.
>
> Paul Speratus, 1484–1551

Exercise

Try to recall the biggest rainbow you have ever seen. Try to recall your most 'real' sacramental experience. Thank God for the waters of baptism which you were offered when you entered the ark of salvation and were signed with the sign of the wood of the cross.

Wednesday 8 December 1999: The Birth of Jesus Is Announced

'Greetings, favoured one! The Lord is with you.' (Luke 1:28)

Today the Church celebrates Mary's own conception and rejoices in the way in which, as the Virgin daughter of Sion, God prepared her to become the mother of the Saviour. We read the story of Jesus's conception.

Scriptural Reading

In the sixth month the angel Gabriel was sent by God
to a town in Galilee called Nazareth, to a virgin engaged
to a man whose name was Joseph, of the house of
David. The virgin's name was Mary. And he came to
her and said, 'Greetings, favoured one! The Lord is
with you.' But she was much perplexed by his words
and pondered what sort of greeting this might be. The
angel said to her, 'Do not be afraid, Mary, for you have
found favour with God. And now, you will conceive in
your womb and bear a son, and you will name him
Jesus. He will be great, and will be called the Son of
the Most High, and the Lord God will give to him the
throne of his ancestor David. He will reign over the
house of Jacob for ever, and of his kingdom there will
be no end.' Mary said to the angel, 'How can this be,
since I am a virgin?' The angel said to her, 'The Holy
Spirit will come upon you, and the power of the Most
High will overshadow you; therefore the child to be
born will be holy; he will be called Son of God. And
now, your relative Elizabeth in her old age has also
conceived a son; and this is the sixth month for her
who was said to be barren. For nothing will be impos-
sible with God.' Then Mary said, 'Here am I, the servant
of the Lord; let it be with me according to your word.'
Then the angel departed from her. (Luke 1:26–38)

Reflection

The New Testament begins with another story of origins. Jesus
was conceived with the consent of Mary. She asks a question,
'How can this be?' and then assents to the angel's message. At
this moment the incarnation begins and from the watery haven
or ark of Mary's body, our salvation is assured. 'He came all so
still', the carol says, reminding us of the simplicity and stillness
of this moment of complete receptivity to the will of God.
Anxiety is cast out; all Mary's misgivings fade away. She

becomes open to the purposes of God and is overshadowed by the Holy Spirit of divine power. The Word becomes flesh in her body.

Mary is an example for all of us, men as well as women, because she is the Christ-bearer. She shows us what it is to bring Jesus into the world. She reminds us that we too can open our hearts to the purposes of God; that we too can be overshadowed by the divine power; that we too can bring forth the Christ Child. As the year gets darker and Christmas approaches, we are reminded that Advent is a season of quiet joy; that we are concerned with silence, and with the work of God which is revealed to us in the most silent and still places of our hearts.

Prayers

We beseech thee, O Lord, pour thy grace into our hearts; that, as we have known the incarnation of thy Son Jesus Christ by the message of an angel, so by his cross and passion we may be brought unto the glory of his resurrection; through the same Jesus Christ our Lord, Amen. (Collect for the Annunciation of the Blessed Virgin Mary, *Book of Common Prayer*)

I sing of a maiden
That is makeless;
King of all kings
To her son she ches.

He came all so still
Where his mother was,
As dew in April
That falleth on the grass.

He came all so still
To his mother's bow'r,
As dew in April
That falleth on the flow'r.

45

He came all so still
Where his mother lay,
As dew in April
That falleth on the spray.

Mother and maiden
Was never none but she:
Well may such a lady
God's mother be.

Medieval carol

There can be nothing which the Holy Spirit can be
said not to have made; and that it cannot be doubted
that all subsists through His operation, whether Angels,
Archangels, Thrones, or Dominions; since the Lord
Himself, whom the Angels serve, was begotten by the
Holy Spirit coming upon the Virgin, as, according to
Matthew, the Angel said to Joseph: 'Joseph, thou son
of David, fear not to take Mary thy wife, for that which
shall be born of her is of the Holy Spirit.' And according
to Luke, he said to Mary: 'The Holy Spirit shall come
upon thee.'

The birth from the Virgin was, then, the work of the
Spirit. The fruit of the womb is the work of the Spirit,
according to that which is written: 'Blessed art thou
among women, and blessed is the Fruit of thy womb.'
The flower from the root is the work of the Spirit, that
flower, I say, of which it was well prophesied: 'A rod
shall go forth from the root of Jesse, and a flower shall
rise from his root.' The root of Jesse the patriarch is the
family of the Jews, Mary is the rod, Christ the flower
of Mary, who, about to spread the good odour of faith
throughout the whole world, budded forth from a virgin
womb, as he himself said: 'I am the flower of the plain,
a lily of the valley.'

The flower, when cut, keeps its odour, and when

46

bruised increases it, nor if torn off does it lose it; so, too, the Lord Jesus, on the gibbet of the cross, neither failed when bruised, nor fainted when torn; and when he was cut by that piercing of the spear, being made more beautiful by the colour of the outpoured Blood, He, as it were, grew comely again, not able in Himself to die, and breathing forth upon the dead the gift of eternal life. On this flower, then, of the royal rod the Holy Spirit rested. (Ambrose of Milan, 339–97, *On the Holy Spirit,* 2.5)

Father,
You prepared the Virgin Mary
To be the worthy mother of your Son.
You let her share beforehand
In the salvation Christ would bring by his death,
And kept her sinless from the first moment of her being.
Help us by her prayers
to live in your presence without sin.
We ask this through our Lord Jesus Christ, your Son,
Who lives and reigns with you and the Holy Spirit,
One God, for ever and ever, Amen.

Collect for the Feast of the Immaculate Conception,
Roman Missal

Exercise

Listen to the words of the angel, 'Hail, favoured one' and prepare yourself to receive the gift of the Christ Child into your very being. Ask what this will mean to you, in your circumstances.

Thursday 9 December 1999: The Messiah Is Promised

'There shall be endless peace for the throne of David and his kingdom.' (Isa. 9:7)

Advent and the coming millennium prepare us for a unique celebration. The dome of heaven is filled with light as the Bible story reaches its climax and all the promises of the Scriptures are fulfilled.

Scriptural Reading

The people who walked in darkness have seen a great light; those who lived in a land of deep darkness – on them light has shined. You have multiplied the nation, you have increased its joy; they rejoice before you as with joy at the harvest, as people exult when dividing plunder. For the yoke of their burden, and the bar across their shoulders, the rod of their oppressor, you have broken as on the day of Midian. For all the boots of the tramping warriors and all the garments rolled in blood shall be burned as fuel for the fire. For a child has been born for us, a son given to us; authority rests upon his shoulders; and he is named Wonderful Counsellor, Mighty God, Everlasting Father, Prince of Peace. His authority shall grow continually, and there shall be endless peace for the throne of David and his kingdom. He will establish and uphold it with justice and with righteousness from this time onward and for evermore. The zeal of the Lord of hosts will do this. (Isa. 9:2–7)

Reflection

There is a mood of expectation that goes with the promise of a Messiah. The Wonderful Counsellor is the Prince of Peace. We are right to experience this sense of anticipation as we enter once again into the mood of the prophet Isaiah. He tells us that the birth of the Messiah is *for* us, that the son is given *to* us. This is no abstracted, disembodied activity on God's part. Jesus engages with our humanity and we are right to feel joyful about this. For in his birth, Jesus initiates something new. He is the Divine Child who calls us all to re-birth and the fulfilment of our potential.

The promise is for us as individuals, for us as a society, for us in our shared church life and for our planet. All of creation is caught up into God's salvific purpose. That is why we recall the birth of Jesus in order to be renewed by it. This year, as we mark two thousand years of God's generosity to us in sending our Messiah to us, we do so with special attention, sharing the belief that renewal is possible, and that it starts with ourselves. Our spiritual needs are met when we turn to God as the source of our joy.

Prayers

Almighty Father,
Give us the joy of your love
To prepare the way for Christ our Lord.
Help us to serve you and one another.
We ask you this through our Lord Jesus Christ, your Son,
Who lives and reigns with you and the Holy Spirit,
One God, for ever and ever, Amen.

Roman Missal

For Christ is King, and Priest, and God, and Lord, and angel, and man, and captain, and stone, and a Son born, and first made subject to suffering, then returning to heaven, and again coming with glory, and he is preached as having the everlasting kingdom: so I prove

49

from all the Scriptures. But that you may perceive what I have said, I quote the words of the Psalm; they are these: 'O God, give Thy judgment to the king, and Thy righteousness unto the king's son, to judge Thy people with righteousness, and Thy poor with judgment. The mountains shall take up peace to the people, and the little hills righteousness. He shall judge the poor of the people, and shall save the children of the needy, and shall abase the slanderer. He shall co-endure with the sun, and before the moon unto all generations. He shall come down like rain upon the fleece, as drops falling on the earth. In his days shall righteousness flourish, and abundance of peace until the moon be taken away. And he shall have dominion from sea to sea, and from the rivers unto the ends of the earth. Ethiopians shall fall down before him, and his enemies shall lick the dust. The kings of Tarshish and the isles shall offer gifts; the kings of Arabia and Seba shall offer gifts; and all the kings of the earth shall worship him, and all the nations shall serve him: for he has delivered the poor from the man of power, and the needy that hath no helper. He shall spare the poor and needy, and shall save the souls of the needy: he shall redeem their souls. (Justin Martyr, c. 100–165, *Dialogue with Trypho*)

The company of the angels and all humanity
Praise the Lord of the earth and the highest heaven.
The high angelic powers and mortals
Rejoice and bless you.
All the creatures of the world adore you as their Lord,
The earth and the sea praise you and pray to you and
    love you.
The stars shining in the sky glorify the Lord;
All your creation gives glory to you, O King.
You sit above the stars at the right hand of the Father on
    high;

Thursday 9 December 1999

O king of heaven, have mercy on us your servants.
Eleventh-century Italian poem

> O come, O come, Emmanuel,
> And ransom captive Israel,
> That mourns in lonely exile here
> Until the Son of God appear:
> *Rejoice! rejoice! Emmanuel*
> *Shall come to thee, O Israel.*
>
> O come, O come, thou Lord of might,
> Who to thy tribes, on Sinai's height,
> In ancient times didst give the law
> In cloud, and majesty, and awe:
>
> O come, thou Rod of Jesse, free
> Thine own from Satan's tyranny;
> From depth of hell thy people save,
> And give them vict'ry o'er the grave:
>
> O come, thou Key of David, come
> And open wide our heav'nly home;
> Make safe the way that leads on high,
> And close the path to misery:
>
> O come, thou Day-spring, come and cheer
> Our spirits by thine advent here;
> Disperse the gloomy clouds of night,
> And death's dark shadows put to flight:
>
> Eighteenth-century Latin, tr. J. M. Neale, 1818–66

Exercise

Say the words of the first verse of 'O come, O come, Emmanuel' out loud. Try saying them in different rooms in your house, out in the street, on the way to work. Notice what you feel in each of these places. Pray now for the Day-spring to well up in you again.

Friday 10 December 1999: The Kingdom of God

'On that day the root of Jesse shall stand as a signal to
the peoples.' (Isa. 11:10)

We prepare ourselves to receive the message that Jesus will
bring: a message of peace and redemption for all people, for
the whole of creation and for our planet.

Scriptural Reading

A shoot shall come out from the stump of Jesse, and a
branch shall grow out of his roots. The spirit of the
Lord shall rest on him, the spirit of wisdom and understanding, the spirit of counsel and might, the spirit of
knowledge and the fear of the Lord. His delight shall
be in the fear of the Lord. He shall not judge by what
his eyes see, or decide by what his ears hear; but with
righteousness he shall judge the poor, and decide with
equity for the meek of the earth; he shall strike the
earth with the rod of his mouth, and with the breath of
his lips he shall kill the wicked. Righteousness shall
be the belt around his waist, and faithfulness the belt
around his loins. The wolf shall live with the lamb, the
leopard shall lie down with the kid, the calf and the
lion and the fatling together, and a little child shall
lead them. The cow and the bear shall graze, their
young shall lie down together; and the lion shall eat
straw like the ox. The nursing child shall play over the
hole of the asp, and the weaned child shall put its hand
on the adder's den. They will not hurt or destroy on all
my holy mountain; for the earth will be full of the

knowledge of the Lord as the waters cover the sea.
(Isa. 11:1–9)

Reflection

The promise is of a kingdom where God will be known and our
own delight will be in the knowledge and love and fear of God.
This is what the incarnation is all about. It is not about a white
Christmas or ice on the Thames or the new dome. It is about
eternal values, ones which can sustain us as we journey into
the next century and the next millennium. The promise of God's
kingdom is awesome. It turns us upside down. It asks what we
really want and offers to deliver it. It says, 'Do you believe in
a theory of human perfectibility where there can be no sin and
all justice will automatically swing into action?' It challenges
us by saying that this is an illusion.

The kingdom which Jesus is and which he inserts into our
midst is hugely real. It knows about human error and sin and
desire; it knows about our mistakes and our troubled hearts and
grievances. It recognises that Utopia cannot be wished into
being. What we have to grapple with is the real world: a world
in which people like us are greedy and heartless and loving and
generous and scared and sinful. If we are prepared to inhabit
this world with a degree of realism, then the kingdom will
come, for we will begin to deal with the fear in our own hearts
and defuse the wider tensions that surround us. We pray for
grace; we pray for light.

Prayers

> All-powerful God,
> Help us to look forward in hope
> To the coming of our Saviour.
> May we live as he has taught,
> Ready to welcome him with burning love and faith.
> We ask this through our Lord Jesus Christ, your Son,
> Who lives and reigns with you and the Holy Spirit,
> One God, for ever and ever, Amen.   *Roman Missal*

Thou whose almighty Word
Chaos and darkness heard,
   And took their flight;
Hear us, we humbly pray,
And where the Gospel-day
Sheds not its glorious ray
   Let there be light!

Thou who didst come to bring
On thy redeeming wing
   Healing and sight,
Health to the sick in mind,
Sight to the inly blind,
Ah! Now to all mankind
   Let there be light!

Spirit of light and love,
Life-giving, holy Dove,
   Speed forth thy flight!
Move on the water's face,
Bearing the lamp of grace,
And in earth's darkest place
   Let there be light!

Blessed and holy Three
Glorious Trinity,
   Wisdom, Love, Might;
Boundless as ocean tide
Rolling in fullest pride,
Through the world far and wide
   Let there be light!

John Marriott, 1780–1825

Lord! Going out from this silence, teach me to be more
alert, humble, expectant, than I have been in the past:
ever ready to encounter you in quiet, homely ways: in
every appeal to my compassion, every act of unselfish

love which shows up and humbles my imperfect love, may I recognise you: still walking through the world. Give me that grace of simplicity which alone can receive your mystery.

Come and abide with me!

Meet me, walk with me!

Enlighten my mind!

And then, Come in! Enter my humble life with its poverty and its limitations as you entered the stable of Bethlehem, the workshop of Nazareth, the cottage of Emmaus.

Bless and consecrate the material of that small and ordinary life.

Feed and possess my soul.

Evelyn Underhill, 1875–1941

Exercise

We pray for the kingdom of God to come. We acknowledge that the Messiah is our King. Ask Jesus to teach you to be more alert, humble, expectant. Ask him today to encounter you in quiet homely ways. Tidy something in your own home – your kitchen or desk drawers, your study or your bedroom. As you impose order there, notice the relationship between right ordering and the coming of the kingdom.

Saturday 11 December 1999: How God Redeems the World

'May you be made strong with all the strength that comes from his glorious power.' (Col. 1:11)

The coming Messiah offers us true freedom and light, because he makes us strong with the utter simplicity of his incarnation and the glorious power of his resurrection, which secure the promise of redemption for us.

Scriptural Reading

He has rescued us from the power of darkness and transferred us into the kingdom of his beloved Son, in whom we have redemption, the forgiveness of sins. He is the image of the invisible God, the firstborn of all creation; for in him all things in heaven and on earth were created, things visible and invisible, whether thrones or dominions or rulers or powers – all things have been created through him and for him. He himself is before all things, and in him all things hold together. He is the head of the body, the church; he is the beginning, the firstborn from the dead, so that he might come to have first place in everything. For in him all the fullness of God was pleased to dwell, and through him God was pleased to reconcile to himself all things, whether on earth or in heaven, by making peace through the blood of his cross. (Col. 1:13–20)

Reflection

We pray to be revealed as the children of light; we pray to enjoy our inheritance as the redeemed of God, as those who have true peace, because we have been rescued from the power of darkness. So first of all we need to ask where darkness lies for us. Then we need to ask how hostile this darkness is. Where do our worst fears lie? What is the greatest source of our distress? Are we anxious about our health; about our relationships; about our past; about our future? Where can Jesus' gift of redemption most closely meet our most pressing concerns? Freedom lies in accepting that Jesus was born for our salvation. What are the ways we can use to prepare ourselves to recall our redemption, as we ask what it means to be children of light? Where is our star? Where does it lie? How is it constellated?

The fullness of God is pleased to dwell in Jesus. God desires to be our fullness too and to know us in the circumstances of our most private and intimate lives, in the places where our concerns are most exposed and we are most needy. In prayer we have to speak to God about our own desire for redemption, not as an abstract concept but as a straightforward bid for peace and love and light and joy in our own circumstances. We believe that Jesus saves us. That is why he was born for us; that is why we await his coming with a genuine sense of hope and expectation. God touches us where we are. This is where we are incarnated. All can be grace.

Prayers

Lord,
Let your glory dawn to take away our darkness.
May we be revealed as the children of light
At the coming of your Son,
Who lives and reigns with you and the Holy Spirit,
One God, for ever and ever, Amen.

Roman Missal

Not yet must we conceive of one Christ in two unconnected states of being, as though the assumption of humanity were merely a function analogous to the guiding of the stars. On the contrary, the one Person is co-extensive with all infinity and all action lies within his scope. Whatever he does, whether it be, or be not, in relation to humanity and in the former case whether it be the exaltation of humanity or the self-emptying of Godhead, is done within the sphere of the Incarnation, the sphere which embraces his whole being and his whole action. The self-emptying itself was not a self-determination, instant and complete, made before in Incarnation, but, as we saw, a process which continued throughout Christ's life on earth and was active to the end. For as he hung, deliberately self-emptied of his glory, on the Cross, he manifested his normal powers by the earthquake shock. His submission to death was the last of a consistent series of exertions of his will, which began with the Annunciation and culminated in the Crucifixion. (Hilary of Poitiers, 315–67, *On the Trinity*, 2)

Christ, whose glory fills the skies,
　　Christ, the true, the only Light,
Sun of Righteousness, arise,
　　Triumph o'er the shades of night;
Day-spring from on high, be near;
Day-star, in my heart appear.

Dark and cheerless is the morn
　　Unaccompanied by thee:
Joyless is the day's return,
　　Till thy mercy's beams I see,
Till they inward light impart,
Glad my eyes and warm my heart.

Visit then this soul of mine;
　　Pierce the gloom of sin and grief;
Fill me, radiancy divine;
　　Scatter all my unbelief;
More and more thyself display,
Shining to the perfect day.

Charles Wesley, 1707–88

Lord Jesus Christ,
For our redemption you were raised up on the wood of the
cross,
So that the whole world, which lay in darkness,
Might be filled with light;
We pray that you will always pour that light
Into our souls and bodies,
So that by it we may come to the light everlasting, Amen.

York Missal I

Exercise

Today is a rest day, a Saturday, a Sabbath day. Find a way in which you can relax, maybe by beating the crowds and doing your Christmas shopping, maybe by sitting around doing nothing.

Week Three: Offertory
Sunday 12 December 1999:
We Offer Ourselves to God

'For all things come from you, and of your own have we given you.' (1 Chr. 29:14)

With the Third Sunday in Advent, the mood of the Church changes; we prepare ourselves joyfully to bring our gifts and our very selves into the presence of God and to be received as we are; and to be blessed for what we have been and will be.

Scriptural Reading

Then David blessed the Lord in the presence of all the assembly; David said: 'Blessed are you, O Lord, the God of our ancestor Israel, for ever and ever. Yours, O Lord, are the greatness, the power, the glory, the victory, and the majesty; for all that is in the heavens and on the earth is yours; yours is the kingdom, O Lord, and you are exalted as head above all. Riches and honour come from you, and you rule over all. In your hand are power and might; and it is in your hand to make great and to give strength to all. And now, our God, we give thanks to you and praise your glorious name.

'But who am I, and what is my people, that we should be able to make this freewill offering? For all things come from you, and of your own have we given you. For we are aliens and transients before you, as were all our ancestors; our days on the earth are like a

shadow, and there is no hope. O Lord our God, all this abundance that we have provided for building you a house for your holy name comes from your hand and is all your own. I know, my God, that you search the heart, and take pleasure in uprightness; in the uprightness of my heart I have freely offered all these things, and now I have seen your people, who are present here, offering freely and joyously to you.'
(1 Chr. 29:10–17)

Reflection

David the King speaks on behalf of the people. He speaks from a full and graced heart. He prays about riches and honour, power and might – the gifts that God wants to give us. He recognises the generosity and abundance of God. He acknowledges that it is only because of this generosity that we can talk about gift and self-offering, about love and freedom and gratitude. Is it surprising then, that when the Son of David, the Messiah, our Saviour, comes, he is both the gift and the giver of gifts?

Yet what counts is not how much we offer to God, nor how much we receive from God; what counts is that our offering should be freely and joyously given; that, in the heart of our humanity, we should receive life from God as generously as Jesus did. What matters is our openness to God and to the loving gifts of the Spirit, so that all we offer back to the Blessed Trinity comes from a free and undivided heart. In the midst of all our trials and traumas, and happiness and joy and renewal, and grief and loss and pain, can we open our hearts to the gift of God and to our own capacity for generosity? Can we thank God for all the divine gifts? At Christmas, shepherds and sages from the East brought gifts to Jesus. Start preparing your gifts now as you open your heart to God's will for you this Christmas and in the new millennium.

Prayers

Lord God,
May we, your people,
Who look forward to the birthday of Christ
Experience the joy of salvation
And celebrate that feast with love and thanksgiving.
We ask this through our Lord Jesus Christ, your Son,
Who lives and reigns with you and the Holy Spirit,
One God, for ever and ever, Amen.

Roman Missal

Nourished by the milk of heaven,
To our tender palates given;
Milk of wisdom from the breast
Of that bride of grace exprest;
By a dewy spirit filled
From fair Reason's breast distilled;
Let us sucklings join to raise
With pure lips our hymns of praise
As our grateful offering,
Clean and pure, to Christ our King.
Let us, with hearts undefiled,
Celebrate the mighty Child.
We, Christ-born, the choir of peace;
We, the people of his love,
Let us sing, nor ever cease,
To the God of peace above.

Clement of Rome, first century,
A Hymn to Christ the Saviour

From glory to glory advancing, we praise thee, O Lord;
thy name with the Father and Spirit be ever adored.

From strength unto strength we go forward on Sion's
highway,
to appear before God in the city of infinite day.

Thanksgiving, and glory and worship, and blessing and
   love,
one heart and one song have the saints upon earth and
   above.

Evermore, O Lord, to thy servants thy presence be nigh;
ever fit us by service on earth for thy service on high.
Liturgy of St James, tr. C. W. Humphreys

Lord of all mercy and goodness, suffer us not by any
ingratitude or hardness of heart to forget the wonderful
benefits that thou hast bestowed upon us this and every
day; but grant that we may be mindful all the days of
our life of the incomparable gifts which thou ever givest
us through Jesus Christ our Lord. (Scottish Prayer)

Exercise
Give someone a present today: a telephone call, flowers, a kiss,
a letter, an e-mail, a message that bears your love. Take note of
the presents that come your way because your friends have
begun to send you Christmas cards that speak of their love for
you.

Monday 13 December 1999:
Following Our Star

'I will go to the altar of God, to God my exceeding
joy.' (Ps. 43:4)

We experience the attraction of Jesus who calls us closer to
him so that we may share in the mystery of his birth. He is the

light from whom we hold our own light. He is the source of all grace. We prepare ourselves to approach his altar, his crib and his cross.

Scripture Reading

Vindicate me, O God, and defend my cause against an ungodly people; from those who are deceitful and unjust deliver me! For you are the God in whom I take refuge; why have you cast me off? Why must I walk about mournfully because of the oppression of the enemy? O send out your light and your truth; let them lead me; let them bring me to your holy hill and to your dwelling. Then I will go to the altar of God, to God my exceeding joy; and I will praise you with the harp, O God, my God. Why are you cast down, O my soul, and why are you disquieted within me? Hope in God; for I shall again praise him, my help and my God. (Ps. 43:1–5)

Reflection

We prepare our gifts; we prepare ourselves, for the gift of the human heart is the greatest offering of all and this is the gift which the celebration of Christmas inspires us to give to God. So we go up to the altar of God. We prepare ourselves for the kind of sacrifices and celebrations which will happen there.

We go up conscious of our humanity, conscious of the fact that we are made in God's image and likeness, and that we are attracted to the source of our very being. The Light of the World is the source of our light. If we are to shine in the dome of heaven, it is only because we mirror the divine image in which we are made. So we need to reflect on how we may be more Christ-like.

What is it about Jesus which most draws us to imitate him? When we look at him, what do we see? A busy Saviour, rushing around doing good? A wise and prudent teacher? A healer? Someone who withdrew to pray and could say of himself, 'I am the Way, the Truth and the Life' because of the intensity of his communion with God? The man who cried when his friend died, and again when he too faced death? The Redeemer of the world? Try to work out which image of Jesus inspires your own spiritual life most powerfully at this time. Let that be the star that calls you out of yourself and invites you to the manger.

Prayers

Lord,
Hear our voices raised in prayer.
Let the light of the coming of your Son
Free us from the darkness of sin.
We ask this through our Lord Jesus Christ, your Son,
Who lives and reigns with you and the Holy Spirit,
One God, for ever and ever, Amen.

Roman Missal

Beyond all measure are things temporal removed from the Eternal, things corporeal from the Incorporeal, things governed from the Governor. For though they possess a wondrous beauty, yet they have no Godhead to be worshipped. That power then, that wisdom, that majesty is to be adored which created the universe out of nothing, and framed by his almighty methods the substance of the earth and sky into what forms and dimensions he willed. Sun, moon, and stars may be most useful to us, most fair to look upon; but only if we render thanks to their Maker for them and worship God who made them, not the creation which does him service. Then praise God, dearly beloved, in all his works and judgements. Cherish an undoubting belief in the Virgin's pure conception. Honour the sacred and Divine mystery of our restoration with holy and sincere service. Embrace Christ born in our flesh, that you may deserve to see him also as the God of glory reigning in his majesty, who with the Father and the Holy Spirit remains in the unity of the Godhead for ever and ever. Amen. (Leo the Great, d. 461, *Sermon* 22, *On the Feast of the Nativity*, 2, 6)

Stars of the morning, so gloriously bright,
filled with celestial resplendence and light,
these that, where night never followeth day,
raise the 'Trisagion' ever and ay:

These are thy counsellors, these dost thou own,
Lord God of Sabaoth, nearest thy throne;
these are thy ministers, these dost thou send,
help of the helpless ones! Man to defend.

These keep the guard amid Salem's dear bowers;
thrones, principalities, virtues, and powers;
where, with the living ones, mystical four,
cherubim, seraphim bow and adore.

'Who like the Lord?' thunders Michael the chief;
Raphael, 'the cure of God', comforteth grief;
and, as at Nazareth, prophet of peace,
Gabriel, 'the light of God', bringeth release.

Then, when the earth was first poised in mid space,
then, when the planets first sped on their race,
then, when were ended the six days' employ,
then all the sons of God shouted for joy.

Still let them succour us; still let them fight,
Lord of angelic hosts, battling for right;
till, where their anthems they ceaselessly pour,
we with the angels may bow and adore.

Joseph the Hymnographer, d. 883, tr. J. M. Neale

We pray you, Lord, look mercifully
And enlighten our hearts with the splendour of your Son's
    incarnation and birth,

His passion, resurrection and ascension,
And the coming of the Holy Spirit;
That we may be strong enough to escape
The darkness of this world,
And, with him as our leader,
May come to our native land
Of eternal glory.

York Missal II

Exercise

Take time to reflect on each of the sacred mysteries you have just prayed about, 'the splendour of your Son's incarnation and birth, his passion, resurrection and ascension, and the coming of the Holy Spirit'. They speak to your deepest desires, to your need for redemption. If you have a Bible, take it out and hold it. Feel how heavy or how light it is; feel the quality of the paper on which it is printed. Smell it. Thank God for it.

Tuesday 14 December 1999:
Preparing Our Gold

'May gold of Sheba be given to him.' (Ps. 72:15)

As we reflect on the gifts we will bring to the manger, we separate out the different bits of our lives. We want to bring our most precious selves to God; we want to acknowledge our need for them too to be redeemed.

Scriptural Readings

 Give the king your justice, O God, and your righteousness to a king's son. Long may he live! May gold of

Sheba be given to him. May prayer be made for him continually, and blessings invoked for him all day long. May there be abundance of grain in the land; may it wave on the tops of the mountains; may its fruit be like Lebanon; and may people blossom in the cities like the grass of the field. May his name endure for ever, his fame continue as long as the sun. May all nations be blessed in him; may they pronounce him happy. (Ps. 72:1, 15–17)

Jesus sat down opposite the treasury, and watched the crowd putting money into the treasury. Many rich people put in large sums. A poor widow came and put in two small copper coins, which are worth a penny. Then he called his disciples and said to them, 'Truly I tell you, this poor widow has put in more than all those who are contributing to the treasury. For all of them have contributed out of their abundance; but she out of her poverty has put in everything she had, all she had to live on.' (Mark 12:41–4)

Reflection

Sometimes we forget how rich we are. Sometimes we forget the richness and abundance which God wills us to enjoy. We may be feeling poor or witless or, in reality – like the widow in Mark's story – we may genuinely be bereft. Yet we are drawn and encouraged by her example, for Jesus commends her for giving her all to God in the coffers of the Temple courtyard. She took no account of her own needs but gave everything to God, including the coins that were her treasure.

Our own personal riches too may only be measured out in coppers, but to God they are infinitely desirable. Our own personal riches may be golden in their intensity; they may shine in the outer world, but to God they too are infinitely desirable. When we recognise our giftedness, we recognise something of the generosity of God as well. So for Christ the King, we prepare a kingly present. Now this is a time of year when many people are preparing their Christmas present lists, and trying to be creative about balancing a Christmas budget. This is an appropriate time of year to be reminded of God's generosity to us and of our own capacity to give from what we have and treasure and value.

What are your gifts? What have you to offer and to give to Christ the King?

Prayers

> Father of love,
> You made a new creation
> Through Jesus Christ your Son.
> May his coming free us from sin
> And renew his life within us,
> For he lives and reigns with you and the Holy Spirit,
> One God, for ever and ever, Amen.

Roman Missal

Let all created things in their loveliness
Give praise;
Let the sun, moon and stars,
The night and the day,
The fields and the seas
Praise the creative wisdom of God's all-providing hand,
Whose glory and power gave them their being.

Let the melodious sounds of our cymbals sing praise
To the saving mercy of his divine and generous wisdom,
Shining brightly before us.
It draws the company of faithful Christians
To seek the beautiful walls and gates of Sion,
Which surpass the fair dwellings of Jacob.

There to his chosen ones
The Blessed Trinity reveals the radiance of his presence.
Perfect peace is there; glory and beauty flourish;

There is found the jewelled hall, the golden folk,
The fragrance of the lily and the deep red rose.

The heavenly Church cries 'Hosanna';
The cherubim and seraphim repeat 'thrice holy'
In eternal glory.
May God's manifold goodness join us to the happy
  company
Of the redeemed, through him who saves all things.

Laudate condita, in *York Missal II*

Take my life, and let it be
consecrated, Lord, to thee;
take my moments and my days,
let them flow in ceaseless praise.
Take my hands, and let them move
at the impulse of thy love.
Take my feet, and let them be
swift and beautiful for thee.

Take my voice, and let me sing
always, only, for my king;
take my lips, and let them be
filled with messages from thee.
Take my silver and my gold;
not a mite would I withhold.
Take my intellect, and use
every power as thou shalt choose.

Take my will, and make it thine:
it shall be no longer mine.
Take my heart: it is thine own;
it shall be thy royal throne.
Take my love; my Lord, I pour
at thy feet its treasure-store.
Take myself, and I will be
ever, only, all for thee.

Frances R. Havergal, 1836–79

Exercise
What can you do this Christmas to give something you value
to the coming Messiah? How can you budget for a hidden gift,
something you give to the poor and needy? Let it cost you; let
it mirror the generosity of God.

Wednesday 15 December 1999: Preparing Our Frankincense

'You shall make an altar on which to offer incense.'
(Exod. 30:1)

'Sacred gifts of mystic meaning/incense doth their God dis-
close.' Today we reflect on all that makes us sacred, all that
makes us hunger and thirst for God. We prepare to offer our
spiritual selves to God.

Scriptural Reading
You shall make an altar on which to offer incense; you
shall make it of acacia wood. It shall be one cubit long,
and one cubit wide; it shall be square, and shall be two
cubits high; its horns shall be of one piece with it. You
shall overlay it with pure gold, its top, and its sides all
around and its horns; and you shall make for it a
moulding of gold all around. And you shall make two
golden rings for it; under its moulding on two opposite
sides of it you shall make them, and they shall hold the
poles with which to carry it. You shall make the poles
of acacia wood, and overlay them with gold. You shall
place it in front of the curtain that is above the ark of
the covenant, in front of the mercy seat that is over the

covenant, where I will meet with you. Aaron shall offer fragrant incense on it; every morning when he dresses the lamps he shall offer it, and when Aaron sets up the lamps in the evening, he shall offer it, a regular incense offering before the Lord throughout your generations. (Exod. 30:1–8)

Reflection

The instructions are detailed: this is how carefully we must prepare the 'mean altar of our heart' to be a place where Jesus is recognised and known and honoured. Incense becomes a symbol of holiness and of prayer, for incense is offered as a sign of our devotion. It curls up into heaven just as our hearts and spirits crave to do as we seek God in the dark and silent time of Advent.

For the message of the Book of Exodus is quite clear: we are preparing a place of encounter. 'I will meet with you', God promises us. Amid the sacred symbols and containers of all that is holy – the ark, the gold moulding, the acacia poles, the mercy seat, the curtain – we are offered an experience of the Divine.

When Jesus was born in a bare manger, the sacred symbols were quite different – the warm breath of animals, the scent of hay, a star-lit night – but the theophany, the encounter with God, was just as intense. Our response to God's desire to be with us is to raise our hearts in prayer and thanksgiving. That is why incense is such a powerful sign of the sacred in our lives. It cuts through our words and our gestures and speaks to our memories and imaginations through direct contact with our senses.

Prayers

Almighty and everlasting God,
by whose Spirit the whole body of the Church
   is governed and sanctified:
hear our prayer which we offer for all your faithful
   people;

that, in their vocation and ministry,
each may serve you in holiness and truth
to the glory of your name;
through our Lord and Saviour Jesus Christ.
Collect of the Second Sunday after Pentecost,
Alternative Service Book 1980

O worship the Lord in the beauty of holiness!
    Bow down before him, his glory proclaim;
with gold of obedience, and incense of lowliness,
    kneel and adore him, the Lord is his name!

Low at his feet lay thy burden of carefulness,
    high on his heart he will bear it for thee,
comfort thy sorrows, and answer thy prayerfulness,
    guiding thy steps as may best for thee be.

Fear not to enter his courts in the slenderness
    of the poor wealth thou wouldst reckon as thine:
truth in its beauty, and love in its tenderness,
    these are the offerings to lay on his shrine.

These though we bring them in trembling and
    fearfulness,
    he will accept for the name that is dear;
mornings of joy give for evenings of tearfulness,
    trust for our trembling and hope for our fear.

O worship the Lord in the beauty of holiness!
    Bow down before him, his glory proclaim;
with gold of obedience, and incense of lowliness,
    kneel and adore him, the Lord is his name!
J. S. B. Monsell, 1811–75

David speaketh thus: *Dirigatur oratio mea sicut incensum* etc.
– Let my prayer be dressed as incense in Thy sight. For even as
incense that is cast into the fire maketh a sweet smell by the
smoke rising up to the air, right so a Psalm savorly and softly

sung or said in a burning heart, giveth up a sweet smell to the face of our Lord Jesus, and to all the Court of Heaven. There dare no flesh-fly rest upon the pot's brink boiling on the fire. Even so can no fleshly delight rest upon a clean soul, that is all bilapped and warmed in the fire of love, boiling and blowing up Psalms and prayers to Jesus. This prayer is always heard of Jesus. It yieldeth grace to Jesus, and receiveth grace again. It maketh a soul familiar, and, as it were, hail-fellow with Jesus, and with all the Angels in Heaven, use it who so can. The work is good and gracious in itself. And though it be not altogether perfect Contemplation in itself, nor the working of love by itself, nevertheless it is in part Contemplation. For why? It cannot be exercised in this manner but by plenty of grace through opening of the spiritual eye. And, therefore, a soul that hath this freedom and this gracious feeling in praying with spiritual savour and heavenly delight hath the grace of Contemplation in the manner as it is.

This prayer is a rich offering filled all with fatness of devotion, received by Angels and presented to the face of Jesus. (Walter Hilton, d. 1396, *The Scale of Perfection*)

> Father,
> May the coming celebration of the birth of your Son
> Bring us your saving help
> And prepare us for eternal life.
> Grant this through our Lord Jesus Christ, your Son,
> Who lives and reigns with you and the Holy Spirit,
> One God, for ever and ever, Amen.
>
> *Roman Missal*

Exercise

Find something with a really interesting and intense smell – some herbs or spices or an orange or a lemon. Breathe in the scent and say 'Let my prayer rise as incense in your sight' as you do so.

Thursday 16 December 1999: Preparing Our Myrrh

'Nicodemus, who had at first come to Jesus by night, also came, bringing a mixture of myrrh and aloes, weighing about a hundred pounds. They took the body of Jesus and wrapped it with the spices in linen cloths, according to the burial custom of the Jews.' (John 19:39–40)

Scriptural Reading

Take the finest spices: of liquid myrrh five hundred shekels, and of sweet-smelling cinnamon half as much, that is, two hundred and fifty, and two hundred and fifty of aromatic cane, and five hundred of cassia – measured by the sanctuary shekel – and a hin of olive oil; and you shall make of these a sacred anointing oil blended as by the perfumer; it shall be a holy anointing oil. With it you shall anoint the tent of meeting and the ark of the covenant, and the table and all its utensils, and the lampstand and its utensils, and the altar of incense, and the altar of burnt-offering with all its utensils, and the basin with its stand; you shall consecrate them, so that they may be most holy; whatever touches them will become holy. You shall anoint Aaron and his sons, and consecrate them, in order that they may serve me as priests. You shall say to the Israelites, 'This shall be my holy anointing oil throughout your generations. It shall not be used in any ordinary anointing of the body, and you shall make no other like it in composition; it is holy, and it shall be holy to you.' (Exod. 30:23–32)

Reflection

> 'Myrrh is mine: its bitter perfume
> tells of his death and Calvary's gloom;
> sorrowing, sighing, bleeding, dying,
> sealed in a stone-cold tomb.'

The familiar words of the carol remind us of the ambivalence with which we prepare this gift during Advent. For our preparation now reminds us of the other purple season in the Church's year, Lent. Advent and Lent cannot be separated from each other; they belong together and are united in the imagery of this strange perfume, myrrh. Myrrh is about priesthood, the gift God gave us when Aaron was anointed. Jesus is the Christ, the anointed Son of God, our great high priest. He stands in the long line of priesthood which represents the true service of God.

But he is also the Temple where God is served: the place of sacrifice and expiation. So myrrh is both celebratory and sacred because it enables us to recognise the priesthood of the Messiah, but also it serves as a shadowy warning. For the Christ who is the anointed one of God will be the sacrifice who redeems us by his death and resurrection.

How do we relate to this troubling gift? How do we prepare ourselves to greet a Messiah who is also a Saviour? One way of doing this is to weigh up the balance of joy and sadness in our own lives, to ask for God's blessing on each of the human moments we live through, and to let go of our unhappiness and pain. For we have been redeemed.

Prayers

> Lord,
> Our sins bring us unhappiness.
> Hear our prayer for courage and strength.
> May the coming of your Son
> Bring us the joy of salvation.
> We ask this through our Lord Jesus Christ, your Son,

Who lives and reigns with you and the Holy Spirit,
One God, for ever and ever, Amen.

Roman Missal

The name of 'Christ' comes from 'chrism'; this name
by which he is called 'Christ' expresses 'unction': nor
were kings and prophets anointed in any kingdom, in
any other place, save in that kingdom where Christ was
prophesied of, where he was anointed, and from whence
the Name of Christ was to come. It is found nowhere
else at all: in no one nation or kingdom. God, then,
was anointed by God; with what oil was he anointed,
but a spiritual one? For the visible oil is in the sign, the
invisible oil is in the mystery; the spiritual oil is within.
God then was anointed for us, and sent unto us; and
God himself was man, in order that he might be
anointed: but he was man in such a way as to be God
still. He was God in such a way as not to disdain to be
man. 'Very man and very God'; in nothing deceitful,
in nothing false, as being everywhere true, everywhere
the Truth itself. God then is man; and it was for this
cause that God was anointed, because God was Man,
and became Christ. (Augustine of Hippo, 354–430,
Exposition on Psalm 45)

White is Thy bearing-cloth, but Thou shalt have a red
    arraying
With blood of all that bare Thy pain, and knew not what
    they bare,
Thy stripes and shames and agonies, Thy wounds and
    guiltless slaying,
The hemlock and the myrrh are Thine, the gall and
    vinegar.
Arise, O Orient Splendour, rise and shine to all men living,
From east and west their cry is heard, their very instant
    cry,

Arabia, Saba, Tharsis kneel, their richest treasures giving,
Stand forth, O Jesus, justified in Thine Epiphany.

Dorothy L. Sayers, 1893–1957,
Catholic Tales and Christian Songs

Your throne, O God, endures forever and ever. Your royal sceptre is a sceptre of equity; you love righteousness and hate wickedness. Therefore God, your God, has anointed you with the oil of gladness beyond your companions; your robes are all fragrant with myrrh and aloes and cassia. From ivory palaces stringed instruments make you glad; daughters of kings are among your ladies of honour; at your right hand stands the queen in gold of Ophir. (Ps. 45:6–9)

Exercise
Rub a little cream or oil into your hands. Experience the way it is absorbed into your skin. Remember Augustine's words: 'visible oil is in the sign, the invisible oil is in the mystery; the spiritual oil is within'.

Friday 17 December 1999: Abiding by Night

'My soul waits for the Lord more than those who watch for the morning.' (Ps. 130:6)

Just as the Magi from the East prepared their gifts, so too did the shepherds. Just as the sheep and lambs gathered strength under the shepherds' care, so did the Lamb of God grow in Mary's womb. We prepare for Christ to come.

Scriptural Reading

'Be dressed for action and have your lamps lit; be like
those who are waiting for their master to return from
the wedding banquet, so that they may open the door
for him as soon as he comes and knocks. Blessed are
those slaves whom the master finds alert when he
comes; truly I tell you, he will fasten his belt and have
them sit down to eat, and he will come and serve them.
If he comes during the middle of the night, or near
dawn, and finds them so, blessed are those slaves. But
know this: if the owner of the house had known at what
hour the thief was coming, he would not have let his
house be broken into. You also must be ready, for the
Son of Man is coming at an unexpected hour.' (Luke
12:35–40)

Reflection

Advent carries more than one meaning for us. We prepare to
renew our sense of the importance of the birth of Jesus and to
understand the mystery of the incarnation with renewed fervour.
But we prepare for another coming too: for each of us will die
and meet God. So too will our universe. The Second Coming is
sometimes portrayed in apocalyptic terms as though the end of
the world were some kind of catastrophe. In the understanding
of the Christian tradition, it is a time of achievement and
fulfilment. We pray that the Master will find us ready; that our
lamps may be burning; that the life of faith may be visible in
us.

A millennium offers the prophets of doom a great run-out.
Is the year 2000 to be an end-time, a time of calamity? Will
computer bugs bring absolute chaos into our world? Or can we
go confidently towards the future and receive it as a gift of
God? The Gospel reminds us that the shepherds were abiding
in the fields by night when they were visited by angels. What
does it mean to us to abide in the present, in the immediate
task, in the present moment, as we prepare for the coming of

our Messiah? The true test of faith lies not in the day, when things are relatively easy for us, but in the long watches of the night. 'Abide in me, as I abide in you,' says Jesus. We pray to abide in his love.

Prayers

O Wisdom of the Most High, ordering all things with
strength and gentleness, come and teach us the way
of truth.

All-powerful Father,
Guide us with your love
As we await the coming of your Son.
Keep us faithful
That we may be helped through life
And brought to salvation.
We ask this through our Lord Jesus Christ, your Son,
Who lives and reigns with you and the Holy Spirit,
One God, for ever and ever, Amen.

Roman Missal

Sleepers, wake! The watch-cry pealeth,
while slumber deep each eyelid sealeth:
awake, Jerusalem, awake!
Midnight's solemn hour is tolling,
and seraph-notes are onward rolling;
they call on us our part to take.
Come forth, ye virgins wise:
the bridegroom comes, arise!
Alleluia!
Each lamp be bright
with ready light
to grace the marriage feast tonight.

Zion hears the voice that singeth,
with sudden joy her glad heart springeth,

at once she wakes, she stands arrayed:
her light is come, her star ascending,
lo, girt with truth, with mercy blending,
her bridegroom there, so long delayed.
All hail! God's glorious son,
all hail! Our joy and crown,
Alleluia!
The joyful call
we answer all,
and follow to the bridal hall.

Praise to him who goes before us!
Let men and angels join in chorus,
let harp and cymbal add their sound.
Twelve the gates, a pearl each portal –
we haste to join the choir immortal
within the holy city's bound.
Ear ne'er heard aught like this,
nor heart conceived such bliss.
Alleluia!
We raise the song,
we swell the throng,
to praise thee ages all along.

Philipp Nicolai, tr. Francis E. Cox

O Jesus, Splendour of eternal glory, Consolation of
the pilgrim soul, with you my lips utter no sound and
to you my silence speaks. How long will my Lord delay
his coming? Let him come to his poor servant and make
him happy. Let him put forth his hand and take this
miserable creature from his anguish. Come, O come,
for without you there will be no happy day or hour,
because you are my happiness and without you my table
is empty. I am wretched, as it were imprisoned and
weighted down with fetters, until you fill me with the
light of your presence, restore me to liberty, and show

81

me a friendly countenance. Let others seek instead of you whatever they will, but nothing pleases me or will please me but you, my God, my Hope, my everlasting Salvation. I will not be silent, I will not cease praying until your grace returns to me and you speak inwardly to me, saying: 'Behold, I am here. Lo, I have come to you because you have called me. Your tears and the desire of your soul, your humility and contrition of heart have inclined me and brought me to you.' (Thomas à Kempis, 1380–1471, *The Imitation of Christ*, 3.21)

> I beseech you
> Be gentle.
> Because, when the flame is lit,
> the wax is consumed quickly.
> When the leaf flowers
> Swift is the withering.
> But if the seed falls
> Into the heart in fallow,
> The passing loveliness,
> The flicker of light,
> Will remain in the dark night,
> To flower with eternal life.
>
> Caryll Houselander, 1901–54, *The Flowering Tree*

Exercise

What are you most afraid of? Think long and hard about this question. Then ask God to take apocalyptic thoughts out of your mind. Let your Messiah say to you: 'Behold, I am here. Lo, I have come to you because you have called me. Your tears and the desire of your soul, your humility and contrition of heart have inclined me and brought me to you.'

Saturday 18 December 1999: Gift of the Heart

'With what shall I come before the Lord, and bow myself before God on high?' (Mic. 6:6)

Micah's question is as pertinent as ever. What difference does belief in God make to the way we live our lives? How does our faith translate into action?

Scriptural Reading

The law of the Lord is perfect, reviving the soul; the decrees of the Lord are sure, making wise the simple; the precepts of the Lord are right, rejoicing the heart; the commandment of the Lord is clear, enlightening the eyes; the fear of the Lord is pure, enduring for ever; the ordinances of the Lord are true and righteous altogether. More to be desired are they than gold, even much fine gold; sweeter also than honey, and drippings of the honeycomb. Moreover by them is your servant warned; in keeping them there is great reward. But who can detect their errors? Clear me from hidden faults. Keep back your servant also from the insolent; do not let them have dominion over me. Then I shall be blameless, and innocent of great transgression. Let the words of my mouth and the meditation of my heart be acceptable to you, O Lord, my rock and my redeemer. (Ps. 19:7–14)

Reflection

The words we speak and the thoughts of our hearts have to match. So too do our actions or deeds. If our hearts seek God and we find our rest in offering them in God's service, then this will show in the way we live. That is why Micah answers his own question by saying: 'What does the Lord require of you but to do justice, and to love kindness, and to walk humbly with your God?' (Mic. 6:8)

As we prepare for Christmas and the coming millennium, as we offer our hearts in gratitude to God, how are we going to 'do justice, love kindness and walk humbly with our God?' There is no generalised answer to this question. Each of us has to find a personal answer, one which fits our circumstances. So for many people this means a re-dedication to the commitments and relationships – at home and at work – which we have already made. For others it will mean opening new doors and adventuring into unknown territory by embracing a cause, by actively giving time and space to help people whom we do not know but who need our help. For others again, it may mean making adjustments to the way we live, so that we take greater care of our planet and our environment.

Prayers

O Ruler of the House of Israel, who gave the law to
Moses on Sinai, come and save us with outstretched arm.

Almighty God,
you have made us for yourself,
and our hearts are restless
till they find their rest in you.
Teach us to offer ourselves to your service,
that here we may have your peace,
and in the world to come may see you face to face;
through Jesus Christ our Lord.

Collect for the Eighteenth Sunday after Pentecost,
Alternative Service Book 1980

In the bleak mid-winter
   frosty wind made moan,
earth stood hard as iron,
   water like a stone:
snow had fallen, snow on snow,
   snow on snow,
in the bleak mid-winter,
   long ago.

Our God, heaven cannot hold him
   nor earth sustain;
heaven and earth shall flee away
   when he comes to reign:
in the bleak mid-winter
   a stable-place sufficed
the Lord God almighty,
   Jesus Christ.

Enough for him, whom cherubim
   worship night and day,
a breast full of milk,
   and a manger full of hay:
enough for him, whom angels
   bow down before,
the ox and ass and camel
   which adore.

Angels and archangels
   may have gathered there,
cherubim and seraphim
   thronged the air –
but only his mother
   in her maiden bliss
worshipped the beloved
   with a kiss.

What can I give him,
   poor as I am?
If I were a shepherd
   I would bring a lamb;
if I were a wise man
   I would do my part;
yet what I can I give him –
   give my heart.

            Christina Rossetti, 1830–94

Great art Thou, O Lord, and greatly to be praised; great is Thy power, and of Thy wisdom there is no end. And man, being a part of Thy creation, desires to praise Thee, man, who bears about with him his mortality, the witness of his sin, even the witness that Thou 'resistest the proud', – yet man, this part of Thy creation, desires to praise Thee. Thou movest us to delight in praising Thee; for Thou hast formed us for Thyself, and our hearts are restless till they find rest in Thee. Lord, teach me to know and understand which of these should be first, to call on Thee, or to praise Thee; and likewise to know Thee, or to call upon Thee. But who is there that calls upon Thee without knowing Thee? For he that knows Thee not may call upon Thee as other than Thou art. Or perhaps we call on Thee that we may know Thee. 'But how shall they call on Him in whom they have not believed? or how shall they believe without a preacher?' And those who seek the Lord shall praise Him. For those who seek shall find Him, and those who find Him shall praise Him. Let me seek Thee, Lord, in calling on Thee, and call on Thee in believing in Thee; for Thou hast been preached unto us. O Lord, my faith calls on Thee, – that faith which Thou hast imparted to me, which Thou hast breathed into me through the incarnation of Thy Son, through the ministry of Thy preacher. (Augustine of Hippo, 354–430, *Confessions*, 1, 1)

Saturday 18 December 1999

All-powerful God,
Renew us by the coming feast of your Son
And free us from our slavery to sin.
Grant this through our Lord Jesus Christ, your Son,
Who lives and reigns with you and the Holy Spirit,
One God, for ever and ever, Amen

Roman Missal

Exercise

'The commandment of the Lord is clear, enlightening the eyes,' the psalmist says. Write down a list of five things which are actively good for you and warm your heart by giving you energy and light. Put your list somewhere safe, as you are going to use it again.

Week Four: Consecration
Sunday 19 December 1999:
John and Jesus

'Holy, holy, holy is the Lord of Hosts.' (Isa. 6:3)

John recognises Jesus as his Lord and Saviour. We too prepare ourselves to recognise our Lord. We approach the holy moment of his birth and presence among us. We join with Mary in saying, 'My soul magnifies the Lord.'

Scriptural Reading

In those days Mary set out and went with haste to a Judean town in the hill country, where she entered the house of Zechariah and greeted Elizabeth. When Elizabeth heard Mary's greeting, the child leapt in her womb. And Elizabeth was filled with the Holy Spirit and exclaimed with a loud cry, 'Blessed are you among women, and blessed is the fruit of your womb. And why has this happened to me, that the mother of my Lord comes to me? For as soon as I heard the sound of your greeting, the child in my womb leapt for joy. And blessed is she who believed that there would be a fulfilment of what was spoken to her by the Lord.' And Mary said, 'My soul magnifies the Lord, and my spirit rejoices in God my Saviour. (Luke 1:39–47)

Reflection

We have greeted God and been greeted in the divine name. We have reflected on our own sinfulness and upon God's forgiveness revealed to us in the great stories of our salvation. We have prepared our gifts. Now, we approach the Holy of Holies, awaiting the moment of the incarnation. Like Elizabeth, we welcome Mary the Mother of Jesus, who wants to come into our homes and our hearts. Like John, the precursor of Christ's birth, we want to recognise our Saviour, however hidden the circumstances in which he appears to us. 'Holy, holy, holy', we greet our Saviour and our God. We leap for joy.

Recognition and proclamation go hand in hand. Once we have known the power and the love of God, we will want to tell other people about it. Once the Spirit has hovered over us and settled upon us and brought Christ to fruition in us, we will want to say, 'My soul magnifies the Lord'. Like John we will embrace the calling that leads us into the wilderness, to the place of preparation, and then to the sacred encounter, to the moment when we can say, 'You yourselves are my witnesses that I said, "I am not the Messiah, but I have been sent ahead of him." For this reason my joy has been fulfilled. He must increase, but I must decrease.'

How is Christ to increase in our lives? How can we lose our self-interest and our pride?

Prayers

Almighty God,
whose servant John the Baptist
was wonderfully born to fulfil your purpose
by preparing the way for the advent of your Son:
lead us to repent according to his preaching
and, after his example,
constantly to speak the truth, boldly rebuke vice,
and patiently suffer for the truth's sake;
through Jesus Christ our Lord. Amen.

Collect for the Feast of John the Baptist,
Alternative Service Book 1980

When a woman is carrying a child she develops a certain instinct of self-defence. It is not selfishness; it is not egoism. It is an absorption into the life within, a folding of self like a little tent around the child's frailty, a God-like instinct to cherish, and some day, to bring forth, the life. A closing upon it like the petals of a flower closing upon the dew that shines in its heart. This is precisely the attitude we must have to Christ, the Life within us, in the Advent of our contemplation.

We could scrub the floor for a tired friend, or dress a wound for a patient in a hospital, or lay the table and wash up for the family; but we shall not do it in martyr spirit or with that worse spirit of self-congratulation, of feeling that we are making ourselves more perfect, more unselfish, more positively kind.

We shall do it just for one thing, that our hands make Christ's hands in our life, that our service may let Christ serve through us, that our patience may bring Christ's patience back to the world. (Caryll Houselander, 1901–54, *The Reed of God*)

> On Jordan's bank the Baptist's cry
> announces that the Lord is nigh;
> awake, and hearken, for he brings
> glad tidings of the king of kings.
>
> Then cleansed be every breast from sin;
> make straight the way for God within;
> prepare we in our hearts a home,
> where such a mighty guest may come.
>
> For thou art our salvation, Lord,
> our refuge, and our great reward;
> without thy grace we waste away,
> like flowers that wither and decay.

To heal the sick stretch out thine hand,
and bid the fallen sinner stand;
shine forth, and let thy light restore
earth's own true loveliness once more.

All praise, eternal Son, to thee
whose advent doth thy people free,
whom with the Father we adore
and Holy Ghost for evermore.
                    Charles Coffin, 1676–1749, tr. J. Chandler

Lord,
Fill our hearts with your love,
And as you revealed to us by an angel
The coming of your Son as man,
So lead us through his suffering and death
To the glory of his resurrection,
For he lives and reigns with you and the Holy Spirit,
One God, for ever and ever, Amen.
                    Roman Missal

Exercise
Think of each of the four characters in this story: Mary,
Elizabeth, John the future Baptist, the unborn Jesus. Imagine
yourself as one of these. Enter into their experience. What does
it feel like to be so profoundly known? Let something within
you leap with joy.

Monday 20 December 1999: Promise and Expectation

'We will see him as he is.' (1 John 3:2)

We stand in the presence of God, ready to receive the fullness of the promise.

Scriptural Reading

See what love the Father has given us, that we should be called children of God; and that is what we are. The reason the world does not know us is that it did not know him. Beloved, we are God's children now; what we will be has not yet been revealed. What we do know is this: when he is revealed, we will be like him, for we will see him as he is. (1 John 3:1–2)

Reflection

The darkness of mystery begins to be tangible to us. We approach the most sacred and holy moment of the birth of our Redeemer. That is why Christmas is so important and not simply a moment of pure joy, or a happy – if slightly fraught – family time, or even a time of bitter loneliness because we happen to have no context in which to celebrate and so we feel deeply isolated.

Our celebration of the incarnation is a moment of recognition, for now the promise of God comes good. We are met as we are by a Redeemer who is like us, and not unlike us. Jesus takes our condition. A ladder is opened between heaven and earth and all creation huddles round with us to receive the warm gift of freedom and redemption. We recognise the Christ Child and he recognises us. We are known by name.

'When he is revealed, we will be like him, for we will see him as he is', John writes. This is true of the moment of the incarnation, when something new will be revealed to us this year as every year; and it is also true of our sense of the Second Coming, when Christ will be revealed in his full glory at the end of our time, and the end of all time. Let it be true too of the eucharistic moments you have this Christmas and with the approach of the New Year. If you are able to receive Communion during this period, let that too be a moment of recognition, when you know your Saviour and are known by him. Then the promise will come true.

Prayers

O Root of Jesse, set up as a sign to the peoples,
come to save us and delay no more.

God of love and mercy,
Help us to follow the example of Mary,
Always ready to do your will.
At the message of an angel
She welcomed your eternal Son
And, filled with the light of your Spirit,
She became the temple of your Word,
Who lives and reigns with you and the Holy Spirit,
One God, for ever and ever, Amen.

Roman Missal

Come, thou redeemer of the earth,
and manifest thy virgin-birth:
let every age adoring fall;
such birth befits the God of all.

Begotten of no human will,
but of the Spirit, thou art still
the word of God in flesh arrayed,
the promised fruit to us displayed.

The virgin womb that burden gained
with virgin honour all unstained;
the banners there of virtue glow;
God in his temple dwells below.

Forth from his chamber goeth he,
that royal home of purity,
a giant in twofold substance one,
rejoicing now his course to run.

From God the Father he proceeds,
to God the Father back he speeds;
his course he runs to death and hell,
returning on God's throne to dwell.

O equal to thy Father, thou!
Gird on thy fleshly mantle now;
the weakness of our mortal state
with deathless might invigorate.

Thy cradle here shall glitter bright,
and darkness breathe a newer light,
where endless faith shall shine serene,
and twilight never intervene.

All laud to God the Father be,
all praise, eternal Son, to thee:
all glory, as is ever meet,
to God the holy Paraclete.

Ambrose, c. 340–97, tr. J. M. Neale

You cannot glory in the Cross of our Lord Jesus Christ
while you trust in treasures laid up on earth: you cannot
taste and see how gracious the Lord is, while you are
hungering for gold. If you have not rejoiced at the
thought of his coming, that day will be indeed a day of
wrath to you.

But the believing soul longs and faints for God; she

94

rests sweetly in the contemplation of him. She glories in the reproach of the Cross, until the glory of his face shall be revealed. Like the Bride, the dove of Christ, that is covered with silver wings (Ps. 68:13), white with innocence and purity, she reposes in the thought of thine abundant kindness, Lord Jesus; and above all she longs for that day when in the joyful splendour of thy saints, gleaming with the radiance of the Beatific Vision, her feathers shall be like gold, resplendent with the joy of thy countenance. Rightly then may she exult, 'his left hand is under my head and his right hand doth embrace me.' The left hand signifies the memory of that matchless love, which moved him to lay down his life for his friends; and the right hand is the Beatific Vision which He hath promised to his own, and the delight they have in his presence. The Psalmist sings rapturously, 'At Thy right hand there is pleasure for evermore' (Ps. 16.11): so we are warranted in explaining the right hand as that divine and deifying joy of his presence. (Bernard of Clairvaux, 1090–1153, *On Loving God,* 4)

Exercise

Make plans about when and where you are going to go to church this Christmas and New Year. Choose carefully and begin to prepare yourself.

Tuesday 21 December 1999: The Census

'But you, O Bethlehem of Ephrathah, who are one of
the little clans of Judah, from you shall come forth for
me one who is to rule in Israel, whose origin is from of
old, from ancient days.' (Mic. 5:2)

> Bethlehem, of noblest cities
>   none can once with thee compare;
> thou alone the Lord from heaven
>   didst for us incarnate bear.

Reality kicks in. The outer world of Roman politics and the
eternal purposes of God meet, as a census brings the Virgin
Mary, Joseph her spouse and Jesus to Bethlehem, where the
Messiah is to be born.

Scriptural Readings

In those days a decree went out from Emperor Augustus
that all the world should be registered. This was the
first registration and was taken while Quirinius was
governor of Syria. All went to their own towns to be
registered. (Luke 2:1–3)

First of all, then, I urge that supplications, prayers, inter-
cessions, and thanksgivings be made for everyone, for
kings and all who are in high positions, so that we may
lead a quiet and peaceable life in all godliness and dignity. This is right and is acceptable in the sight of God
our Saviour, who desires everyone to be saved and to
come to the knowledge of the truth. (1 Timothy 2:1–4)

Reflection

The early Christian community reckoned that the purposes of God and our own purposes, even those of our totally secular world, can meet. They believed that the Emperor Augustus and the Governor Quirinius were agents of God in our world, because they oversaw the birth of Jesus, in the sense that their census ensured that the prophecy of Micah would be fulfilled. Jesus would be born in Bethlehem because of the intervention of a totally arbitrary force, the edict of a Roman Emperor. God is alive and active, present in all things, absent from none.

So too with our own celebration of Christmas. The Christian churches hold the memory of the incarnation in the life of faith-filled communities and individuals, as well as in stone and prayers and carols and songs. The birth of Jesus is a public event. That is why we call people to come to church at Christmas; we offer the hope and fulfilment of belief; we offer the knowledge of redemption. Without interaction with the outer world, without our churches and our worship, which make a kind of interface between the world of censuses and political reality and the inner world of grace, the invitation would be empty and in vain. It would look arbitrary and esoteric, the outreach of some little sect.

So we rely on the public signs of two thousand years of Christianity, even while we explore and dwell on its inner meaning. We need to thank God for the census and, in our own times, for a calendar based on the birth of Christ – however odd its reading of times and dates. Bizarre though it seems, we even need to thank God for commercial pressures willing us to spend, spend, spend; for a Post Office mailing system; for bank holidays; for turkeys and plum pudding; for the infrastructure of Christmas. The celebration of Christmas is a wonderful example of the way in which God seeks us out where we are and not apart from it. Believe it or not, the construction of a millennium dome is also an extraordinary marker, for whatever its secular status, it serves to remind us all that Jesus was born and lives for us now. In the outer and public world, people want to celebrate, whatever their beliefs. In the inner and private world, that is also true, however ambivalent we feel about the relationship between the way in which the birth of Jesus is greeted and received. So yes, we buy our Christmas trees and lights and crackers, we get in the parsnips and sprouts. We lash out on drinks and presents and parties.

God meets us here: within the celebration and not apart from it. The census is a reminder that the divine and the human interact. God's purposes are genuinely worked out within our world.

Prayers

> O Key of David, who opens the gates of the eternal
> kingdom, come to liberate from prison the captive
> who lives in darkness.

Lord,
Hear the prayers of your people.
May we who celebrate the birth of your Son as man
Rejoice in the gift of eternal life when he comes in glory,
For he lives and reigns with you and the Holy Spirit,
One God, for ever and ever, Amen.

Roman Missal

God is working his purpose out as year succeeds to year,
God is working his purpose out and the time is drawing
    near;
Nearer and nearer draws the time, the time that shall
    surely be,
when the earth shall be filled with the glory of God as
    the waters cover the sea.

From utmost east to utmost west where'er man's foot
    hath trod,
by the mouth of many messengers goes forth the voice
    of God,
'Give ear to me, ye continents, ye isles, give ear to me,

that the earth may be filled with the glory of God as the
  waters cover the sea.'

All we can do is nothing worth unless God blesses the
  deed;
vainly we hope for the harvest-tide till God gives life to
  the seed;
yet nearer and nearer draws the time, the time that shall
  surely be,
when the earth shall be filled with the glory of God as
  the waters cover the sea.

Arthur Campbell Ainger, 1841–1919

This vision was shewed, to mine understanding, for
that our Lord would have the soul turned truly unto the
beholding of him, and generally of all his works. For
they are full good; and all his doings are easy and sweet,
and to great ease bringing the soul that is turned from
the beholding of the blind Deeming of man unto the
fair sweet Deeming of our Lord God. For a man beholdeth some deeds well done and some deeds evil,
but our Lord beholdeth them not so: for as all that hath
being in nature is of Godly making, so is all that is
done, in property of God's doing. For it is easy to
understand that the best deed is well done: and so well
as the best deed is done – the highest – so well is the
least deed done; and all thing in its property and in the
order that our Lord hath ordained it to from without
beginning. For there is no doer but he.

    I saw full surely that he changeth never his purpose
in no manner of thing, nor never shall, without end.
For there was no thing unknown to him in his rightful
ordinance from without beginning. And therefore all-
thing was set in order ere anything was made, as it
should stand without end; and no manner of thing shall
fail of that point. For he made all things in fulness of

goodness, and therefore the blessed Trinity is ever full pleased in all his work.

And all this shewed he full blissfully, signifying thus: 'See! I am God: see! I am in all thing: see! I do all thing: see! I lift never mine hands off my works, nor ever shall, without end: see! I lead all thing to the end I ordained it to from without beginning, by the same Might, Wisdom and Love whereby I made it. How should any thing be amiss?' *(*Julian of Norwich, c. 1342–after 1413, *Revelations of Divine Love,* Third Revelation, Chapter Eleven)

When it was time for you to appear on earth, O Lord, the first census had been ordered: it was then that you willed to write down the names of the future believers in your birth. The order had come from Caesar Augustus: but your everlasting Kingdom also was renewed. Wherefore we, too, offer you what is better than taxes and money: rightful theology expressed in hymn and verse. O God, save our souls!

Feast of the Nativity: Lauds, *Byzantine Daily Worship*

Exercise

'God is working his purpose out.' Buy some Christmas crackers or new decorations. Let yourself be thoroughly secular and enjoy the way in which God brings all our worlds together in the service of grace. As Julian of Norwich noted, 'How should anything be amiss?'

Wednesday 22 December 1999: The Journey

'Joseph also went from the town of Nazareth in Galilee to Judea, to the city of David called Bethlehem, because he was descended from the house and family of David. He went to be registered with Mary, to whom he was engaged and who was expecting a child.' (Luke 2:4–5)

The gospel narrative tells us that Mary and Joseph make their way to Bethlehem, where the Child of the promise will be born. The historical references in this narrative take us right back to the beginning of salvation history.

Scriptural Reading

And the servant said, 'O Lord, God of my master Abraham, please grant me success today and show steadfast love to my master Abraham. I am standing here by the spring of water, and the daughters of the townspeople are coming out to draw water. Let the girl to whom I shall say, "Please offer your jar that I may drink", and who shall say, "Drink, and I will water your camels" – let her be the one whom you have appointed for your servant Isaac. By this I shall know that you have shown steadfast love to my master.'

Before he had finished speaking, there was Rebekah, who was born to Bethuel son of Milcah, the wife of Nahor, Abraham's brother, coming out with her water jar on her shoulder. The girl was very fair to look upon, a virgin, whom no man had known. She went down to the spring, filled her jar, and came up. Then the servant ran to meet her and said, 'Please let me sip a little water

101

from your jar.' 'Drink, my lord,' she said, and quickly lowered her jar upon her hand and gave him a drink. When she had finished giving him a drink, she said, 'I will draw for your camels also, until they have finished drinking.' So she quickly emptied her jar into the trough and ran again to the well to draw, and she drew for all his camels. The man gazed at her in silence to learn whether or not the Lord had made his journey successful.

When the camels had finished drinking, the man took a gold nose-ring weighing a half-shekel, and two bracelets for her arms weighing ten gold shekels, and said, 'Tell me whose daughter you are. Is there room in your father's house for us to spend the night?' She said to him, 'I am the daughter of Bethuel son of Milcah, whom she bore to Nahor.' She added, 'We have plenty of straw and fodder and a place to spend the night.' The man bowed his head and worshipped the Lord. (Gen. 24:12–26)

Reflection

Abraham sends his servant to find a wife for his beloved son, Isaac. Beside the well, at the source of all spiritual energy, the servant sees an un-bedecked girl, a virgin daughter of the people, who offers water to him and to the animals. He puts bracelets and rings upon her, consecrating her for the divine service. He accepts straw and fodder and a place to spend the night. He bows his head and worships God because the journey he has made is at an end: salvation comes to the tribe and offspring of Abraham. Like Joseph, the servant serves a greater purpose. He is swept into the journey God calls us each to make: the journey towards greater faith and intimacy with the divine.

How can we trust this journey in an uncertain world and as the millennium approaches? Are you a Joseph, the servant of a greater project than your own? Are you like Abraham, the great patriarch who hopes and prays that all will be well, yet has to rely on other people to see the will of God realised? Are you like Mary, burdened and near to term, aching for your child to be born? Are you a Rebekah figure, brought in from the outside, a spectator, and now suddenly a participant in the drama of salvation? Are you like the well, deep and secure, a place of refreshment to which other people can come? Or are you like the camels: animals who do their bit and do their best, enjoying the dispensation of salvation, without quite knowing why? The water in the well is offered to us all.

Prayers

O Morning star, radiance of eternal light, sun of
  justice, come and enlighten those who live in
    darkness and in the shadow of death.

Bethlehem, make ready, for Eden has been opened for all; Ephrata, be alert, for the Tree of Life has blossomed forth from the Virgin in the cave. Her womb has become a spiritual paradise wherein the divine Fruit was planted – and if we eat of it, we shall live and not die like Adam. Christ is coming forth to bring back to life the likeness that had been lost in the beginning.

Troparion of the Preparation,
Byzantine Daily Worship

Father, hear the prayer we offer:
  not for ease that prayer shall be,
but for strength that we may ever
  live our lives courageously.

Not for ever in green pastures
  do we ask our way to be;
but the steep and rugged pathway
  may we tread rejoicingly.

Not for ever by still waters
  would we idly rest and stay;
but would smite the living fountains
  from the rocks along our way.

Be our strength in hours of weakness,
in our wanderings be our guide;
through endeavour, failure, danger,
Father, be thou at our side.

Maria Willis, 1824–1908

Jesus said to the Samaritan woman, 'Everyone who drinks of this water will be thirsty again, but those who drink of the water that I will give them will never be thirsty. The water that I will give will become in them a spring of water gushing up to eternal life.' The woman said to him, 'Sir, give me this water, so that I may never be thirsty or have to keep coming here to draw water.' (John 4:13–15)

Eternal God,
whose Son Jesus Christ
is the way, the truth, and the life:
grant us to walk in his way,
to rejoice in his truth,
and to share his risen life;
who is alive and reigns with you and the Holy Spirit,
one God, now and for ever, Amen.

Collect of the Third Sunday before Lent,
Alternative Service Book 1980

Exercise

If you can, go for a walk today. Imagine the journey of Mary and Joseph. Think about the gift of water, the well of salvation and renewal that lies at the end of the journey, with the birth of the coming Messiah. When you get home, turn on the taps in your kitchen and feel the water and the promise of new life that it brings.

Thursday 23 December 1999: The Innkeeper

'Then he put him on his own animal, brought him to an inn, and took care of him.' (Luke 10:34)

The innkeeper becomes an unwitting player in the drama of our salvation. There is no room in the inn but it still remains a place of hospitality and rest so that shelter is found for the family from Nazareth.

Scriptural Reading

'Then the king will say to those at his right hand, "Come, you that are blessed by my Father, inherit the kingdom prepared for you from the foundation of the world; for I was hungry and you gave me food, I was thirsty and you gave me something to drink, I was a stranger and you welcomed me." Then the righteous will answer him, "Lord, when was it that we saw you hungry and gave you food, or thirsty and gave you something to drink?" And the king will answer them, "Truly I tell you, just as you did it to one of the least of these who are members of my family, you did it to me."' (Matt. 25:34–40)

Reflection

We do not understand the consequences of our actions. We do not know how we fit into the designs of God. The innkeeper is an unknown player. But we remember him because, when Mary and Joseph completed their journey to Bethlehem, there was no room for them in the inn. But he offered them, and their unborn child, the shelter of a stable: 'I was a stranger and you welcomed me.'

As our Christmas preparations come together; as we do our final shopping and checking; as we dust down the crib, we reflect on the ways in which the secular and the sacred come together in our own lives. Christmas is an odd mix of them both. Can we live with that, or are we tempted to keep the two apart? Where is our inn? Where is our place of shelter for the ambivalent in our lives? Where do we have enjoyment and also protection; where do we give hospitality and also repose? If we are unable to receive him there, because there is no room for him, where do we make a space for him?

These sound like moralistic questions, ones which divide our experience into good bits and bad bits. The action of God in Christ cuts through our anxieties about 'getting Christmas right' or about ensuring that our hearts are open to his message. For what God does in the incarnation is mirrored and illustrated in what happens to the unborn child, when there is no room for him. He goes to the space beyond all the spaces we make for ourselves or even for him. He does a new thing, and the world is refreshed and saved by this. A new dispensation is proclaimed as our Saviour comes to a stable.

There is a further dimension though. Two thousand years after the birth of Jesus, there are still people for whom there is no room in the inn, nor any real stable where they may rest. The world is full of refugees and displaced people. Pray for them this Christmas.

Prayers

O King of the peoples, and corner-stone of the
Church, come and save the people whom you made from
the dust of the earth.

At that time, since Mary was of the house of David,
she registered with the Venerable Joseph in Bethlehem.
She was with child, having conceived virginally. Her
time was come and they could find no room in the inn,
but the cave seemed a joyful palace for the Queen.

Christ is born to renew the likeness that had been lost of old. The earth offers a cave to God, the Inaccessible one. (Kontakion of the Preparation, *Byzantine Daily Worship*)

> Love divine, all loves excelling,
>   Joy of heaven, to earth come down,
> fix in us thy humble dwelling,
>   all thy faithful mercies crown.
> Jesu, thou art all compassion,
>   pure unbounded love thou art;
> visit us with thy salvation,
>   enter every trembling heart.
>
> Come, almighty to deliver,
>   let us all thy grace receive;
> suddenly return, and never,
>   never more thy temples leave.
> Thee we would be always blessing,
>   serve thee as thy host above;
> pray, and praise thee, without ceasing,
>   glory in thy perfect love.
>
> Finish then thy new creation:
>   pure and spotless let us be;
> let us see thy great salvation,
>   perfectly restored in thee;
> changed from glory into glory,
>   till in heaven we take our place,
> till we cast our crowns before thee,
>   lost in wonder, love, and praise.

Charles Wesley, 1707–88

He was the son of David, so was He also the Lord of David. And as He was from Abraham, so did He also exist before Abraham. And as He was the servant of God, so is He the Son of God, and Lord of the universe.

And as He was spit upon ignominiously, so also did He breathe the Holy Spirit into His disciples. And as He was saddened, so also did He give joy to His people. And as He was capable of being handled and touched, so again did He, in a non-apprehensible form, pass through the midst of those who sought to injure Him, and entered without impediment through closed doors. And as He slept, so did He also rule the sea, the winds, and the storms. And as He suffered, so also is He alive, and life-giving, and healing all our infirmity. And as He died, so is He also the Resurrection of the dead. He suffered shame on earth, while He is higher than all glory and praise in heaven; who, 'though He was crucified through weakness, yet He liveth by divine power', who 'descended into the lower parts of the earth', and who 'ascended up above the heavens'; for whom a manger sufficed, yet who filled all things; who was dead, yet who liveth for ever and ever. Amen. (Irenaeus, c. 130–200, *Fragments from the Lost Writings*)

Father,
We contemplate the birth of your Son.
He was born of the Virgin Mary
And came to live among us.
May we receive forgiveness and mercy
Through our Lord Jesus Christ, your Son,
Who lives and reigns with you and the Holy Spirit,
One God, for ever and ever, Amen.

Roman Missal

Exercise
Think about the humility of God, who accepts our humanity and offers us a new way of living. Use the words 'fix in us thy humble dwelling' to help you to pray. Ask Jesus to find new places in your heart where he can come to life. Ask yourself what you most need. Try to do something restful today.

Friday 24 December 1999: The Waiting Manger

'Today you will know that the Lord is coming to save you and in the morning you will see his glory.' (Exod. 16:6–7)

Gentle silence awaits us as we come near to the stable and to the manger. Amid the frenzied Christmas preparations and last-minute shopping, we are offered a place of safety and of stillness, where the Divine Child may be born in us.

Scriptural Readings

The vision of Isaiah son of Amoz, which he saw concerning Judah and Jerusalem in the days of Uzziah, Jotham, Ahaz, and Hezekiah, kings of Judah. Hear, O heavens, and listen, O earth; for the Lord has spoken: I reared children and brought them up, but they have rebelled against me. The ox knows its owner, and the donkey its master's crib; but Israel does not know, my people do not understand. (Isa. 1:1–3)

For while gentle silence enveloped all things, and night in its swift course was now half gone, your all-powerful word leapt from heaven, from the royal throne, into the midst of the land that was doomed. (Wisdom of Solomon 18:14–15a)

Reflection

This is a moment of welcome and disclosure. In the darkness, Jesus will be born anew in us. He comes to us where we are and offers us the transformation we most desire, the transformation that will make us more real, more human and, ultimately, more Christlike.

What does this mean in practice? This year, as every year, we are offered a new beginning, a new start, and rather than tying it to the millennium or to New Year's Day, the gospel offers it to us today. For we can open our hearts to receive the mighty warrior who leaps down from heaven, the Word who wants to be made flesh within our flesh.

Today we can pin our hopes on the promise of God. 'The ox knows its owner, and the donkey its master's crib': the animals turn to God and experience the dawn of salvation from on high. Christmas Eve is a sacred time, for its very darkness visits our fears of loss and abandonment. Yet it is the moment when our anxiety and longing are most truly met. 'Fear not', the angel said to Mary. Today, and especially tonight, we hear those words as they are spoken into our lives, and we too are called to allow the Christ Child to be born in the manger of our hearts.

Prayers

> O Emmanuel, our king and lawgiver, come and save
> us, Lord our God.

Almighty God and Father of light,
A child is born for us and a son is given for us.
Your eternal Word leaped down from heaven in the silent
    watches of the night,
And now your Church is filled with wonder at the nearness
    of God.
Open our hearts to receive his life
And increase our vision with the rising of the dawn,
That our lives may be filled with his glory and his peace,
who lives and reigns for ever and ever, Amen.

Roman Missal

> Now then I pray you accept his Conception, and leap
> before him; if not like John from the womb, yet like

David, because of the resting of the Ark. Revere the enrolment on account of which thou wast written in heaven, and adore the Birth by which thou wast loosed from the chains of thy birth, and honour little Bethlehem, which hath led thee back to Paradise; and worship the manger through which thou, being without sense, wast fed by the Word. Know as Isaiah bids thee, thine Owner, like the ox, and like the ass thy Master's crib. (Gregory Nazianzen, 329–89, *Selected Orations*, 17)

Drop down, ye heavens, from above, and let the skies pour down righteousness.

Be not wroth very sore, O Lord, neither remember iniquity for ever: thy holy cities are a wilderness, Sion is a wilderness, Jerusalem a desolation: our holy and our beautiful house, where our fathers praised thee.

We have sinned, and are as an unclean thing, and we all do fade as a leaf: and our iniquities, like the wind, have taken us away; thou hast hid thy face from us: and hast consumed us, because of our iniquities.

Ye are my witnesses, saith the Lord, and my servant whom I have chosen: that ye may know me and believe me: I, even I, am the Lord, and beside me there is no saviour: and there is none that can deliver out of my hand.

Comfort ye, comfort ye my people; my salvation shall not tarry: I have blotted out as a thick cloud thy transgressions: fear not, for I will save thee: for I am the Lord thy God, the holy one of Israel, thy redeemer.
The Advent Prose (*Rorate Caeli*)

Exercise

On the First Sunday of Advent you drew a star and were asked where you would pin it. Tonight a star shines down upon you. Where do you most want its rays to find you? Where do you most need the graces of Christmas to touch your life? Turn your insights into a prayer; pray for the light of this star. Some time in the evening, try to use these words:

> God our Father,
> Tonight you have made known to us again
> the power and coming of our Lord Jesus Christ;
> may our Christmas celebration
> confirm our faith and fix our eyes on him
> until the day dawns
> and Christ the Morning Star
> rises in our hearts.
> To him be glory both now and for ever, Amen.
>
> Collect at Eucharist of Christmas Night,
The Promise of his Glory

Saturday 25 December 1999: Jesus Is Born

'And the Word became flesh and lived among us, and we have seen his glory, the glory as of the Father's only Son, full of grace and truth.' (John 1:14)

Our Advent watch is over and Christmas can begin. We have waited faithfully for the past four weeks, praying that our Messiah would find us ready on the great day of his birth. Enjoy all that he offers you today.

Scriptural Reading

But you, O Bethlehem of Ephrathah, who are one of the little clans of Judah, from you shall come forth for me one who is to rule in Israel, whose origin is from of old, from ancient days. Therefore he shall give them up until the time when she who is in labour has brought forth; then the rest of his kindred shall return to the people of Israel. And he shall stand and feed his flock in the strength of the Lord, in the majesty of the name of the Lord his God. And they shall live secure, for now he shall be great to the ends of the earth; and he shall be the one of peace. (Mic. 5:2–5a)

Reflection

'And he shall be the one of peace.' The Saviour whom we greet today offers us peace. He comes among us in glory, and totally redefines what glory means, for he is born as a helpless baby. So the mighty arm he stretches out for our salvation 'in the strength of the Lord' is pitifully little and small.

The new-born Jesus puts everything in perspective. He reminds us of our humanity and of the generosity of God in holding us in being. He deflates our own ideas of grandeur and self-importance, by coming among us as a little one, a child. He opens the gate of heaven to the weak and to infants, to people who can become 'as little children'. Do not be afraid to find comfort and consolation in being childlike this Christmas. Enjoy what it brings you. Savour what you eat and drink. Turn on the lights of your mental Christmas tree and let them shine for you as well as for other people.

This is a day of comfort and rejoicing. Let the 'majesty of the name of the Lord your God' lighten your step and fill your heart, for today we become the children of God 'by adoption and by grace'.

Prayers

Almighty God, who hast given us thy only-begotten Son to take our nature upon him, and as at this time to be born of a pure Virgin; grant that we being regenerate, and made thy children by adoption and grace, may daily

be renewed by thy Holy Spirit; through the same our
Lord Jesus Christ, who liveth and reigneth with thee
and the same Spirit, ever one God, world without end,
Amen.

Collect for Christmas Day,
Book of Common Prayer

A dry rod lacking moisture's dew,
In a manner strange and new,
Bears both fruit and flowers too,
Like the maiden-mother chaste.

This fruit is her blessed child,
Fruit of gladness undefiled;
Adam had not been beguiled
If this fruit he'd chanced to taste.

Gracious Saviour of all lands,
Held in Mary's loving hands,
Though your throne in heaven stands
In a stable here you rest.

Through this child to us now given,
May our sins be all forgiven;
Help us, who on earth have striven
And by perils are oppressed.

Virga sicca, part of the Sequence
Missus Gabriel in *York Missal II*

We pray you, O God,
Graciously to cleanse our souls
And our consciences,
That as Christ comes to our hearts
He may find them made ready for himself.

Precamur nostras in *York Missal II*

Father,
We are filled with the new light
By the coming of your Word among us.
May the light of faith
Shine in our words and actions.
Grant this through our Lord Jesus Christ, your Son,
Who lives and reigns with you and the Holy Spirit,
One God, for ever and ever, Amen.

Roman Missal

Exercise

He came all so still,
where his mother lay,
as dew in April
that falleth on the spray.

Find a still moment today and savour it. Let the Morning Star
rise in your heart.

Week Five: Communion
Sunday 26 December 1999:
Mary, the Mother of Jesus

'Sing and rejoice, O daughter of Zion! For lo, I will come
and dwell in your midst, says the Lord.' (Zech. 2:10)

Mary rejoices and rests after the birth of her baby. Let today be
a happy and a restful day for you. We come to communion with
our God.

Scriptural Reading

And Mary said, 'My soul magnifies the Lord, and my
spirit rejoices in God my Saviour, for he has looked with
favour on the lowliness of his servant. Surely, from now
on all generations will call me blessed; for the Mighty
One has done great things for me, and holy is his name.
His mercy is for those who fear him from generation to
generation. He has shown strength with his arm; he has
scattered the proud in the thoughts of their hearts. He
has brought down the powerful from their thrones, and
lifted up the lowly; he has filled the hungry with good
things, and sent the rich away empty. He has helped his
servant Israel, in remembrance of his mercy, according
to the promise he made to our ancestors, to Abraham
and to his descendants for ever.' (Luke 1:46–55)

Reflection

Mary's song of praise is directed to God. Today we reflect on her place in the story of salvation. We observe her as she rests and enjoys her baby. We listen to her as her heart sings to God. She is the Virgin Daughter of Zion who fulfils the promise and brings forth the Messiah.

Today we look forwards to the celebration of the millennium and we look backwards to the events of Jesus's birth. Mary can be the linchpin who brings these two events together, for her story is all about receptivity, about greeting God in the circumstances of our everyday lives, about knowing him when he comes to us. Her Magnificat is hugely hopeful; it is a song that sings with a brand new message. The birth of the Messiah offers the possibility of change because it reverses the values by which we run our lives. Our prejudices and our ideologies are unmasked and undermined. From now on, the ways we understand our world and also the gospel have to be re-examined. We need new thinking for a new age and Mary, the Mother of God can bring values and concerns into our lives which will make a difference.

She calls for a reversal of values and offers men and women alike a new way of working with and for God. Today she rests and enjoys and receives the visitors who come to see her baby. Our moment of communion with Mary and her child stabilises us. So we rest in it.

Prayers

Let us pray
That Mary, the mother of the Lord,
Will help us by her prayers.
God our Father,
May we always have the prayers
Of the Virgin Mother Mary,
For through Jesus Christ her Son,
You bring us life and salvation,
For he lives and reigns with you and the Holy Spirit,
One God, for ever and ever, Amen.

Roman Missal

Little Jesus, sweetly sleep, do not stir;
we will lend a coat of fur,
we will rock you, rock you, rock you,
we will rock you, rock you, rock you:
see the fur to keep you warm,
snugly round your tiny form.

Mary's little baby, sleep, sweetly sleep,
sleep in comfort, slumber deep;
we will rock you, rock you, rock you,
we will rock you, rock you, rock you:
we will serve you all we can,
darling, darling little man.

Percy Dearmer, 1867–1936

First Point. The first Point is to see the persons; that is, to see Our Lady and Joseph and the maid, and, after His Birth, the Child Jesus, I making myself a poor creature and a wretch of an unworthy slave, looking at them and serving them in their needs, with all possible respect and reverence, as if I found myself present; and then to reflect on myself in order to draw some profit.

Second Point. The second, to look, mark and contemplate what they are saying, and, reflecting on myself, to draw some profit. (Ignatius of Loyola, 1491–1556, *Spiritual Exercises,* Reflection on the Nativity)

The blossoming rose which is Mary
Springs from the tainted stem of our first mother Eve:
She rises like the morning star amid the heavenly
    constellations,
Fair as the moon.
Her fragrance surpasses every kind of balsam, spice of
    incense:

She is purple as the violet, dewy as the rose, white as
   the lily.
The divine offspring of the most high Father chose her,
That he might take his holy flesh from her pure virgin
   body . . .

O woman, truly holy and lovable,
From whom sprang our redemption,
The salvation of the world, and true life,

You are the Father's darling,
You are the gracious mother of Jesus,
You are the temple of the Holy Spirit.

A Rea Virga, York Missal II

Exercise
Think about the Christmas presents you got yesterday. Thank
God for them and pray for each of the people who gave them to
you. Show them to Mary and offer them for the service of her
Child. Think of your own mother and pray for her today. This is
a moment of communion. Welcome it as such.

Monday 27 December 1999: Joseph

'Jesus came to his home town and began to teach the
people in their synagogue, so that they were astounded
and said, 'Where did this man get this wisdom and
these deeds of power? Is not this the carpenter's son?'
(Matt. 13:54–5)

Joseph, the most silent of the participants in the nativity scene, is a model for us. His influence on Jesus is unimaginable and it begins right at the moment of his birth.

Scriptural Reading

Now the birth of Jesus the Messiah took place in this way. When his mother Mary had been engaged to Joseph, but before they lived together, she was found to be with child from the Holy Spirit. Her husband Joseph, being a righteous man and unwilling to expose her to public disgrace, planned to dismiss her quietly. But just when he had resolved to do this, an angel of the Lord appeared to him in a dream and said, 'Joseph, son of David, do not be afraid to take Mary as your wife, for the child conceived in her is from the Holy Spirit. She will bear a son, and you are to name him Jesus, for he will save his people from their sins.' (Matt. 1:18–21)

Reflection

Our attention has been fixed on Jesus and Mary. Today we remember Joseph. He is described as a righteous man. He becomes a model for all righteous men, for all those who want to serve God and live honourably. What does this mean? Joseph is in touch with his inner world. He is someone to whom God can speak in a dream. He is sensitive to the messages which he hears while he sleeps. Like John the Baptist, he is content to decrease whilst Jesus increases in wisdom and knowledge and the love and fear of God. True communion with God exposes us to new and previously unimaginable experiences. So Joseph is set to be an invisible yet highly influential role in Jesus's life. He models the love of God the Father to him. He mediates the will of God to his Son. Joseph is a model for every father, every mother, for he restores our faith and confidence in benign parenting.

When he thought he should dismiss his wife, because of the child she was carrying, he wanted to do so 'quietly'. Yet with the intervention of his dream, this strong and quiet man took on a new role and new dignity. He protected and saved the

Messiah and became the person who taught Jesus how to say, 'Abba' or Father. The Christian community cannot thank Joseph enough for that. So Father becomes a strong and a quiet word; a word we can use with confidence; a word which will bring us also into that spiritual and divine world where our dreams will speak to us of God's will. When we think about Joseph, we acknowledge the power and strength and comfort of a good man, we experience a kind of communion with his experience – and thank God for that.

Prayers

> God our Father,
> who from the family of your servant David
> raised up Joseph the carpenter
> to be the guardian of your incarnate Son
> and husband of the Blessed Virgin Mary:
> give us grace to follow him
> in faithful obedience to your commands;
> through Jesus Christ your Son, our Lord
> who is alive and reigns with you, in the unity of the
> Holy Spirit,
> one God, for ever and ever, Amen.

Collect for the Feast of St Joseph,
The Christian Year

> Sons are indeed a heritage from the Lord, the fruit of the
> womb a reward. Like arrows in the hand of a warrior are
> the sons of one's youth. Happy is the man who has his
> quiver full of them. He shall not be put to shame when
> he speaks with his enemies in the gate. Happy is every-
> one who fears the Lord, who walks in his ways. You
> shall eat the fruit of the labour of your hands; you shall
> be happy, and it shall go well with you. Your wife will
> be like a fruitful vine within your house; your children
> will be like olive shoots around your table. Thus shall
> the man be blessed who fears the Lord. (Ps. 128:3–4)

There is a general rule concerning all special graces granted to any human being. Whenever the divine favour chooses someone to receive a special grace, or to accept a lofty vocation, God adorns the person chosen with all the gifts of the Spirit needed to fulfil the task at hand.

This general rule is especially verified in the case of St Joseph, the foster-father of our Lord and the husband of the Queen of our world, enthroned above the angels. He was chosen by the eternal Father as the trustworthy guardian and protector of his greatest treasures, namely, his divine Son and Mary, Joseph's wife. He carried out this vocation with complete fidelity until at last God called him, saying: 'Good and faithful servant, enter into the joy of the Lord'.

In him the Old Testament finds its fitting close. He brought the noble line of the patriarchs and prophets to its promised fulfilment. What the divine goodness had offered as a promise to them, he held in his arms. Obviously, Christ does not now deny to Joseph that intimacy, reverence and very high honour which he gave him on earth, as a son to his father. Rather we must say that in heaven Christ completes and perfects all that he gave at Nazareth. (Bernadine of Siena, 1380–1444, *Sermons*)

O nations, let us be eager and celebrate the nativity of Christ. Let us lift up our minds and hearts to Bethlehem, and imagine the Virgin on her way to the cave to give birth to the Lord of All, our God, the stupendous Wonder Joseph contemplated and took for a mere human child wrapped in swaddling clothes. But when he had seen all, he became certain the Child was the true God who grants mercy to our soul. (Vespers for Christmas, *Byzantine Daily Worship*)

Exercise
Ask God to bless your dreams and to speak to you through them. If you can, have a little nap today.

Tuesday 28 December 1999: The Shepherds

'The one who enters by the gate is the shepherd of the sheep. The gatekeeper opens the gate for him, and the sheep hear his voice. He calls his own sheep by name and leads them out.' (John 10:2–3)

Jesus comes to his own. As the Son of David, he is a shepherd-king. Small wonder then that the angels told of his birth to shepherds who were abiding in their fields by night. At the manger, he is visited by shepherds.

Scriptural Reading

Therefore, you shepherds, hear the word of the Lord: As I live, says the Lord God, because my sheep have become a prey, and my sheep have become food for all the wild animals, since there was no shepherd; and because my shepherds have not searched for my sheep, but the shepherds have fed themselves, and have not fed my sheep; therefore, you shepherds, hear the word of the Lord: Thus says the Lord God, I am against the shepherds; and I will demand my sheep at their hand, and put a stop to their feeding the sheep; no longer shall the shepherds feed themselves. I will rescue my sheep from their mouths, so that they may not be food for them. For thus says the Lord God: I myself will search for my sheep, and will seek them out. I will feed them with good pasture, and the mountain heights of Israel shall be their pasture; there they shall lie down in good grazing land, and they shall feed on rich pasture on the mountains of Israel. I myself will be the shepherd of my sheep, and I will make them lie down, says the Lord God. (Ezek. 34:7–11, 14–15)

Reflection

The prophet Ezekiel writes despairingly of the work of the shepherds of God's people. They have been unfaithful and have not looked after their sheep. So God is to send another shepherd: one who will search out the lost and take care of the flock; one who will enable them to lie down and rest. 'The Lord is my shepherd, I shall not want,' we pray.

The promise is fulfilled when Jesus is born in Bethlehem. That is why shepherds are the first to be called 'by night' to come to the crib and to recognise him. They come from darkness into the light and experience the joy that goes with welcoming the Child of the promise. The imagery in this story is deep with symbolism as we are reminded that the whole of creation, the night and the day, the mountains, hills and fields, the animals and the whole of humanity are called into the story of the incarnation, because the Saviour has come to us all and calls us into relationship with each other.

What looks like a simple story set on a hillside is an account of the far-reaching effects of the salvation God offers us in Jesus. 'My shepherd is the Lord,' we pray and ask to be brought to the Christ Child with faith-filled hearts, like the shepherds.

Prayers

Praise to you, O faithful God!
You never fail those who trust in you,
but you let them share your glory.
You fight for us against everything
That could attack us and do us harm.
You are our shepherd,
you free us from the snare.
You protect us who revere you, O God;
Great is the sweetness that you give us.

Christus hunc diem, ninth century

See amid the winter's snow,
born for us on earth below;
see the tender Lamb appears,
promised from eternal years:

Hail, thou ever-blessed morn!
Hail, redemption's happy dawn!
Sing through all Jerusalem,
Christ is born in Bethlehem.

Lo, within a manger lies
he who built the starry skies;
he who, throned in height sublime,
sits amid the cherubim:

Say, ye holy shepherds, say
what your joyful news today;
wherefore have ye left your sheep
on the lonely mountain steep?

'As we watched at dead of night,
lo, we saw a wondrous light;
angels singing "Peace on earth"
told us of the Saviour's birth.'

Sacred infant, all divine,
what a tender love was thine,
thus to come from highest bliss
down to such a world as this!

Teach, O teach us, Holy Child,
by thy face so meek and mild,
teach us to resemble thee,
in thy sweet humility:

Hail, thou ever-blessed morn!
Hail, redemption's happy dawn!
Sing through all Jerusalem,
Christ is born in Bethlehem.

Edward Caswall, 1814–78

We can forsooth if we be true lovers of our Lord Jesu Christ, think upon him when we walk, and hold fast the song of his love whiles we sit in fellowship; and we may have mind of him at the board and also in tasting of meat and drink. At every morsel of meat and draught of drink we ought to praise God, and in time of our meat taking and the space betwixt morsels to yield him praising with honey sweetness and a mental cry, and to yearn with desire while at meat. And if we be in labour of our hands what lets us to lift our hearts to heaven and without ceasing to hold the thought of endless love? And so in all time of our life, being quick and not slow, nothing but sleep shall put our hearts from him.

O what joy and gladness glides into the love? O with how happy and truly desirable sweetness it fulfils his soul? Love certain is life without end, abiding where it is set and made firm in Christ. When this love after loving desire is rooted in the heaven, neither prosperity nor adversity may change it, as the wisest men have written. Then no marvel it shall turn the night to day, darkness to light, heaviness to melody, noy to solace, and labour to sweet rest. This love truly is not of imagination or feigned, but true and perfect, and given to Christ without parting, yielding angel's song with melody to Jesu. (Richard Rolle, 1300–49, *The Fire of Love*)

> David was chosen God's servant,
> Called from the sheepfold
> And brought from his flocks
> To shepherd God's people Jacob.
> David tended them with care,
> David led them with a firm hand.
>
> Ps. 78:70–3

Exercise

Pray to the shepherd-king. 'If we be in labour of our hands what lets us to lift our hearts to heaven and without ceasing to hold the thought of endless love?' Richard Rolle asks. Let the shepherds teach you how to pray at work and at play, so that you too can hear the angel's song and hail redemption's happy dawn. Ask the angels to visit you and give you good tidings of great joy. What is the most joyful message you could hear today?

Wednesday 29 December 1999: The Sheep

'For he is our God, and we are the people of his pasture, and the sheep of his hand. O that today you would listen to his voice!' (Ps. 95:7)

As our communion deepens with Jesus, Mary and Joseph, with the shepherds and the sheep whom they guard on the hillside, with the whole of creation as it groans for redemption, so we are brought inexorably to contemplate the destiny of the Lamb of God, who takes away the sins of the world.

Scriptural Reading
'I am the good shepherd. The good shepherd lays down his life for the sheep. The hired hand, who is not the shepherd and does not own the sheep, sees the wolf coming and leaves the sheep and runs away – and the wolf snatches them and scatters them. The hired hand runs away because a hired hand does not care for the sheep. I am the good shepherd. I know my own and my own know me, just as the Father knows me and I know the Father. And I lay down my life for the sheep. I have other sheep that do not belong to this fold. I must bring them also, and they will listen to my voice. So there will be one flock, one shepherd.' (John 10:11–16)

Reflection

'The good shepherd lays down his life for the sheep.' What does this mean in reality? It means that the destiny of Jesus was held in the Father's care from the very moment of his birth. He is the perfect lamb who takes away the sins of the world. No further sacrifice is required. All that is needed is that we recognise the relationship between the manger and the cross. Both are made of wood and both call Jesus to offer himself in love.

Salvation is a personal gift as well as a gift offered to the whole world. As we prepare for the new millennium, we are going to need to be quite focused and centred. We are going to need to be aware of the cosmic significance of salvation, but also of our own redemption. Jesus was born as our Messiah, the elect and anointed of God. He was born as our Saviour and he continues to save us. We can turn to him with utter confidence and trust at this time. The world is saved by the Lamb who takes away its sin. The cosmos is saved. But so too are we and, at this time, when everything is being painted on the big canvas of people's hopes and fears for the millennium, we must not lose sight of the personal gift of God to us. We are known and loved in our individuality, in the personal anxiety or courage which we experience. 'Behold the Lamb of God, behold him who takes away the sins of the world.'

Prayers

God of peace,
who brought again from the dead our Lord Jesus Christ,
that great shepherd of the sheep,
by the blood of the eternal covenant:
make us perfect in every good work to do your will,
and work in us that which is well-pleasing in your sight;
through Jesus Christ our Lord. Amen.

Collect for Third Sunday of Easter,
Alternative Service Book 1980

128

Loving shepherd of thy sheep,
keep thy lamb, in safety keep;
nothing can thy power withstand,
none can pluck me from thy hand.

Loving Saviour, thou didst give
thine own life that we might live,
and the hands outstretched to bless
bear the cruel nails' impress.

I would praise thee every day,
gladly all thy will obey,
like thy blessed ones above
happy in thy precious love.

Loving shepherd, ever near,
teach thy lamb thy voice to hear;
suffer not my steps to stray
from the straight and narrow way.

Where thou leadest I would go,
walking in thy steps below,
till before my Father's throne
I shall know as I am known.

Jane E. Leeson, 1807–82

Look up now, weak wretch, and see what thou art. What art thou, and what hast thou merited, thus to be called of our Lord? What weary wretched heart, and sleeping in sloth, is that, the which is not wakened with the draught of this love and the voice of this calling! Beware, thou wretch, in this while with thine enemy; and hold thee never the holier nor the better, for the worthiness of this calling and for the singular form of living that thou art in. But the more wretched and cursed, unless thou do that in thee is goodly, by grace and by counsel, to live after thy calling. And insomuch thou shouldest be more meek and loving to thy ghostly spouse, that He that is the Almighty God, King of Kings and Lord of Lords, would meek Him so low unto thee, and amongst all the flock of His sheep so graciously would choose thee to be one of His specials, and sithen set thee in the place of pasture, where thou mayest be fed with the sweetness of His love, in earnest of thine heritage the Kingdom of Heaven. (Anon, fourteenth century, *The Cloud of Unknowing*, 2)

Exercise

Sheep are noisy creatures. If you live near them you cannot but be aware of them. You watch them as they change, for they inhabit the cycle of the seasons with a strange intensity, providing now meat and now wool. Take the risk of doing something seasonal today. Try to be a winter creature, do something to experience the cold and then enjoy the warmth of your heating system, your equivalent of warm wool. Thank God for the experience and for the warmth of salvation.

Thursday 30 December 1999: The Message

'But the angel said to them, "Do not be afraid; for see – I am bringing you good news of great joy for all the people: to you is born this day in the city of David a Saviour, who is the Messiah, the Lord." ' (Luke 2:10–11)

It takes time for the message of Christmas to sink in. We are offered new life and the promise of hope as we prepare for the beginning of a new century and a new millennium.

Scriptural Reading

Blessed be the God and Father of our Lord Jesus Christ, who has blessed us in Christ with every spiritual blessing in the heavenly places, just as he chose us in Christ before the foundation of the world to be holy and blameless before him in love. He destined us for adoption as his children through Jesus Christ, according to the good pleasure of his will, to the praise of his glorious grace that he freely bestowed on us in the Beloved. In him we have redemption through his blood, the forgiveness of our trespasses, according to the riches of his grace that he lavished on us. With all wisdom and insight he has made known to us the mystery of his will, according to his good pleasure that he set forth in Christ, as a plan for the fullness of time, to gather up all things in him, things in heaven and things on earth. In Christ we have also obtained an inheritance, having been destined according to the purpose of him who accomplishes all things according to his counsel and will, so that we, who were the first to set our hope on Christ, might live for the praise of his glory. In him you also, when you had heard the word of truth, the gospel of your salvation, and had believed in him, were marked with the seal of the promised Holy Spirit; this is the pledge of our inheritance towards redemption as God's own people, to the praise of his glory. (Eph. 1:3–14)

Reflection

The message of Jesus cuts across all our expectations. Jesus Christ meets our desire to live for ever. We are loved and saved and desired. God embraces us and calls us to enjoy salvation. When we celebrate Christmas, this is what we remember. But if we feel flat after Christmas, we are reminded that there is more to the Christian memory than we imagine.

On the night before he died, the day on which Jesus ate his

final meal with his friends, on a Thursday like today, Maundy Thursday, he pledged himself to us and asked us to pledge ourselves to him. 'Do this in memory of me,' he said. That is how we can live for the 'pledge of his redemption'. That is how we are 'marked with the seal of the promised Holy Spirit'.

What can we do in memory of him? How can we take bread, bless it, break it and share it with those whom we love? How can we share the message of Jesus, the good news? How, on a winter's day, a day of expectation, can we move beyond ritual to genuine celebration? How can we live comfortably and honourably under the dome of heaven? The Scripture reading gives us an answer. We are asked to live for the 'praise of his glory'. That is our destiny. Like all the characters who gather in the stable and who worship at the manger, we are asked for something simple and given something overwhelming. We are asked to commit ourselves to the new life represented by this baby and we are asked to do so in the full knowledge that he will die for our salvation. The story of Jesus is compressed, so that the beginning and middle and end are all available to us if we listen to his message: he loves us and is our Saviour, we need have no fear.

Prayers

> Of the Father's love begotten
>   ere the worlds began to be,
> he is Alpha and Omega,
>   he the source, the ending he,
> of the things that are, that have been,
>   and that future years shall see,
>   evermore and evermore.
>
> At his word they were created;
>   he commanded; it was done:
> heaven and earth and depths of ocean
>   in their threefold order one;
> all that grows beneath the shining

of the light of moon and sun,
    evermore and evermore.

O that birth for ever blessed!
    When the Virgin, full of grace,
by the Holy Ghost conceiving,
    bare the saviour of our race,
and the babe, the world's redeemer,
    first revealed his sacred face,
        evermore and evermore.

O ye heights of heaven, adore him;
    angel-hosts, his praises sing;
powers, dominions, bow before him,
    and extol our God and king:
let no tongue on earth be silent,
    every voice in concert ring,
        evermore and evermore.

This is he whom seers and sages
    sang of old with one accord;
whom the writings of the prophets
    promised in their faithful word;
now he shines, the long-expected:
    let creation praise its Lord,
        evermore and evermore.

Hail, thou judge of souls departed!
    Hail, thou king of them that live!
On the Father's throne exalted
    none in might with thee may strive;
who at last in judgement coming
    sinners from thy face shalt drive,
        evermore and evermore.

Christ, to thee, with God the Father,
    and, O Holy Ghost, to thee,
hymn and chant and high thanksgiving

and unwearied praises be,
honour, glory, and dominion,
and eternal victory,
evermore and evermore.

Prudentius, 348–410,
tr. J. M. Neale, H. W. Baker and others

Almighty God,
in Christ you make all things new.
Transform the poverty of our nature
by the riches of your grace,
and in the renewal of our lives
make known your heavenly glory;
through Jesus Christ our Lord.

Collect of the Fourth Sunday after Epiphany,
Alternative Service Book 1980

I make the wonderful carven beams
Of cedar and of oak
To build King Solomon's house of dreams,
With many a hammer-stroke,
And the gilded, wide-winged cherubims.

I have no thought in my heart but this:
How bright will be my bower
When all is finished; my joy it is
To see each perfect flower
Curve itself up to the tool's harsh kiss.

How shall I end the thing I planned?
Such knots are in the wood!
With quivering limbs I stoop and stand,
My sweat runs down like blood . . .
I have driven the chisel through my hand.

Dorothy L. Sayers, 1893–1957,
'The Carpenter's Son'

Exercise

At the beginning of Advent, you drew a star and thought of
where you wanted to put it. Where is your star now? On the
Saturday a week before Christmas, you thought about things
which are good for you. Are they still good for you now? Reflect
on both these exercises and see if they can help you feel your
way towards a do-able New Year resolution. Try to be as realistic
as possible and pray for the mystery of the Good News to shine
on your choices.

Friday 31 December 1999: Celebration

'And you shall hallow the fiftieth year and you shall
proclaim liberty throughout the land to all its inhabi-
tants. It shall be a jubilee for you: you shall return,
every one of you, to your property and every one of
you to your family.' (Lev. 25:10)

God recognises our need to mark time with celebrations. We
are invited to proclaim liberty and to return to our roots.
Practically speaking, we are also asked to restore other people
to theirs. In this way we can face the future with confidence
and hope.

Scriptural Reading

Therefore be imitators of God, as beloved children, and
live in love, as Christ loved us and gave himself up for
us, a fragrant offering and sacrifice to God.

For once you were darkness, but now in the Lord
you are light. Live as children of light – for the fruit of

the light is found in all that is good and right and true. Try to find out what is pleasing to the Lord. Take no part in the unfruitful works of darkness, but instead expose them. For it is shameful even to mention what such people do secretly; but everything exposed by the light becomes visible, for everything that becomes visible is light. Therefore it says, 'Sleeper, awake! Rise from the dead, and Christ will shine on you.' (Eph. 5: 1, 2, 8–14)

Reflection

The invitation is clear: we are invited to inhabit the light, to be light and to live in love. These words speak to our deepest sense of self, to our desire to shine for God and for each other. So we are given a vision of splendour and freedom as we face the turning of the year, the century, the millennium. We are promised consolation.

The passing of time has always fascinated people. Yet we fear end-time, and a millennium panders to our fears. Is this year's ending going to overtake and consume us? Are we part of the culture of death which feels overwhelmed by the rolling years? How are we to take heart and to embrace the future confidently? How are we to receive this as a moment of communion, an intense experience of the incarnation and redemption, a genuine celebration of the fact that Jesus was born and died for us and that he invites us to party with him now? How can we be renewed like the phoenix?

The Letter to the Ephesians offers us an answer by linking the life of faith with the saving mystery of the resurrection. Today we are offered a resurrection experience, an opportunity to invest our hope and energy in the future. 'Sleeper, awake! Rise from the dead, and Christ will shine on you.'

Prayers

O Almighty God, who alone art without variableness
or shadow of turning, and hast safely brought
us through the changes of time to the beginning of
another year; we beseech thee to pardon the sins
we have committed in the year which is past, and give
us grace that we may spend the remainder of our days
to thy honour and glory; through Jesus Christ our
Lord, Amen. (*A Free Church Book of Common
Prayer*)

O God, our help in ages past,
    our hope for years to come,
our shelter from the stormy blast,
    and our eternal home;

Beneath the shadow of thy throne
    thy saints have dwelt secure;
sufficient is thine arm alone,
    and our defence is sure.

Before the hills in order stood,
    or earth received her frame,
from everlasting thou art God,
    to endless years the same.

A thousand ages in thy sight
    are like an evening gone,
short as the watch that ends the night
    before the rising sun.

Time, like an ever-rolling stream,
    bears all its sons away;
they fly forgotten, as a dream
    dies at the opening day.

O God, our help in ages past,
    our hope for years to come,

> be thou our guard while troubles last,
> and our eternal home.
>
> Isaac Watts, 1674–1748

Let us consider that wonderful sign of the resurrection which takes place in Eastern lands, that is, in Arabia and the countries round about. There is a certain bird which is called a phoenix. This is the only one of its kind, and lives five hundred years. And when the time of its dissolution draws near that it must die, it builds itself a nest of frankincense, and myrrh, and other spices, into which, when the time is fulfilled, it enters and dies. But as the flesh decays a certain kind of worm is produced, which, being nourished by the juices of the dead bird, brings forth feathers. Then, when it has acquired strength, it takes up that nest in which are the bones of its parent, and bearing these it passes from the land of Arabia into Egypt, to the city called Heliopolis. And, in open day, flying in the sight of all men, it places them on the altar of the sun, and having done this, hastens back to its former abode. The priests then inspect the registers of the dates, and find that it has returned exactly as the five hundredth year was completed. (Clement of Alexandria, 150–215, *First Epistle*, 25)

Almighty God,
who wonderfully created us in your own image
and yet more wonderfully restored us
through your Son Jesus Christ:
grant that, as he came to share in our humanity,
so we may share in the life of his divinity;
who is alive and reigns with you and the Holy Spirit
one God, now and for ever, Amen.

Collect for the Sunday after Christmas Day,
Alternative Service Book 1980

Friday 31 December 1999

An affirmation of faith to be said as midnight approaches –

> Let there be
> Respect for the earth,
> Peace for its people
> Love in our lives
> Delight in the good
> Forgiveness for past wrongs
> And from now on, a new start.
>> Council of Churches for Britain and Ireland

A scriptural reflection on this prayer –

The earth is the Lord's. (Ps. 24:1)
Seek peace and ensure it. (Ps. 34:14)
Mercy and truth are met together. (Ps. 85:10)
Flee from evil, and do the thing that is good. (Ps. 37:27)
Blessed is he whose unrighteousness is forgiven. (Ps. 32:1)
So teach us to number our days, that we may apply our
  hearts unto wisdom. (Ps. 90:12)

Prepared by Leslie Burnham

Exercise
'Try to find out what is pleasing to the Lord.' Yesterday you
began to work on a realistic New Year's resolution. Offer it to
the Lord today and take the risk of writing it down somewhere
in your new diary. Then – if you can – go out and celebrate!

Saturday 1 January 2000: New Beginnings

'After eight days had passed, it was time to circumcise the child; and he was called Jesus, the name given by the angel before he was conceived in the womb.' (Luke 2:21)

A new year begins, a new century and a new millennium. We thank God and pray for a sense of renewal. May newness enter the very core of our being. May the star that led the Magi to the manger lead us forward in confidence and hope as we witness the dawn of a new era.

Scriptural Reading

So if anyone is in Christ, there is a new creation: everything old has passed away; see, everything has become new! All this is from God, who reconciled us to himself through Christ, and has given us the ministry of reconciliation; that is, in Christ God was reconciling the world to himself, not counting their trespasses against them, and entrusting the message of reconciliation to us. So we are ambassadors for Christ, since God is making his appeal through us; we entreat you on behalf of Christ, be reconciled to God. For our sake he made him to be sin who knew no sin, so that in him we might become the righteousness of God.

As we work together with him, we urge you also not to accept the grace of God in vain. For he says, 'At an acceptable time I have listened to you, and on a day of salvation I have helped you.' See, now is the acceptable time; see, now is the day of salvation! (2 Cor. 5:17–6:2)

Reflection

Now is the day of salvation. Two thousand years of Christian history roll over and we are offered a brand new beginning, a fresh opportunity to reflect on the ever ancient and ever new meaning of salvation. To God a thousand years are but a day. The past and the next thousand years are held in God's hand. We are safe because we live within God's time and not simply in our own. All is grace to the children of the day, the children of the light.

So how are we to live as children of the light? How are we to act out the message of reconciliation? Paul calls the community at Corinth to be ambassadors for Christ. We too take up a ministry of reconciliation, bent on sharing with other people what we have learnt ourselves, namely that God knows and loves and forgives us, whatever we have done; that Jesus was born for our salvation; that the Spirit hovers over our world, illuminating our faith. We live within the dispensation of grace.

Reconciliation is to be our hallmark. This means that we have to be very serious about building community, both within our intimate relationships and within the groups to which we belong by nature or by grace. That is why Paul calls this a ministry, a way of telling other people about the saving work of God.

Now is a day of salvation, as was yesterday, as tomorrow will be. Everything has become new because we celebrate our redemption. The star leads us forward to contemplate the meaning of what we experience.

Prayers

Lord of the ages,
You are our beginning and our end.
Everlasting God, we place our days within your care.
Eternal Father, we trust you.
For your faithfulness in the past, we thank you;
For your constant care we praise you;

For our future in your love, we place ourselves
Into your keeping and offer our lives for your service;
Through Jesus Christ, your eternal Son,
Our Saviour.

Patterns and Prayer for Christian Worship,
Baptist Union of Great Britain

The heavens declare thy glory, Lord;
in every star thy wisdom shines;
but when our eyes behold thy word,
we read thy name in fairer lines.

Sun, moon, and stars convey thy praise
round the whole earth, and never stand;
so, when thy truth began its race,
it touched and glanced on every land.

Nor shall thy spreading gospel rest
till through the world thy truth has run;
till Christ has all the nations blest
that see the light or feel the sun.

Great sun of righteousness, arise;
bless the dark world with heavenly light;
thy gospel makes the simple wise,
thy laws are pure, thy judgements right.

Thy noblest wonders here we view,
in souls renewed and sins forgiven:
Lord, cleanse my sins, my soul renew,
and make thy word my guide to heaven.

Isaac Watts, 1674–1748

And I saw the holy city, the new Jerusalem, coming
down out of heaven from God, prepared as a bride
adorned for her husband. And I heard a loud voice from
the throne saying, 'See, the home of God is among
mortals. He will dwell with them as their God; they

will be his peoples, and God himself will be with them; he will wipe every tear from their eyes. Death will be no more; mourning and crying and pain will be no more, for the first things have passed away.'

And the one who was seated on the throne said, 'See, I am making all things new.' Also he said, 'Write this, for these words are trustworthy and true.' Then he said to me, 'It is done! I am the Alpha and the Omega, the beginning and the end. To the thirsty I will give water as a gift from the spring of the water of life.' (Rev. 21:2–6)

Almighty God and Father,
The human birth of your only-begotten Son
Was the beginning of new life.
May he set us free from the tyranny of sin.
We make our prayer through Jesus Christ our Lord,
    Amen.

The Divine Office

Exercise

Do something which will help newness enter the very core of your being. You will know what this thing should be: burning old letters, chucking out old clothes or toys. Be realistic. Let go of the past in a spontaneous way. Find a way of putting your trust in God.

Week Six: Dismissal
Sunday 2 January 2000:
Renewal of Our Hope

'By awesome deeds you answer us with deliverance, O God of our salvation; you are the hope of all the ends of the earth and of the farthest seas.' (Ps. 65:5)

The three virtues of faith, hope and charity are integral to the Christian life. Today we consider hope, because our own is under pressure, either to hope for the wrong things or to despair. God renews us and offers us a covenant.

Scriptural Reading

The days are surely coming, says the Lord, when I will make a new covenant with the house of Israel and the house of Judah. It will not be like the covenant that I made with their ancestors when I took them by the hand to bring them out of the land of Egypt – a covenant that they broke, though I was their husband, says the Lord. But this is the covenant that I will make with the house of Israel after those days, says the Lord: I will put my law within them, and I will write it on their hearts; and I will be their God, and they shall be my people. No longer shall they teach one another, or say to each other, 'Know the Lord,' for they shall all know me, from the least of them to the greatest, says the Lord; for I will forgive their iniquity, and remember their sin no more. (Jer. 31:31–4)

Reflection

At the beginning of Advent we remembered that this central liturgical season was a time of expectation and hope; that it offered us the opportunity to reflect on the incarnation of Jesus and on his work of redemption for the salvation of the world. With the coming of a New Year, we are also promised new hope and a new destiny. The three Christian virtues of faith, hope and charity have a timeless appeal. Today we put hope first for, on one level, it is the virtue which is most under attack in a world which searches for meaning away and apart from God.

Where is your hope focused? The prophet Jeremiah gives us a timeless message. He says that God alone gives us a firm basis for hope. We are not left dangling in the air with vain promises: we are given a vision to live by: a dome which is set in heaven and not one of our own making. The wording sounds austere when you first read it. 'I will put my law within them, and I will write it on their hearts.' Is this an intrusive God, one who gets through the cracks into our personal psyche? Or is there a promise here? Is this what the covenant really means? That God wants and intends to be in relationship with us. 'I will be their God, and they shall be my people.' Whatever is offered here echoes across thousands of years of history. We have a timeless promise, a promise for today. That is why we can be hopeful.

Prayers

> O God,
> by whose command the order of time runs its course:
> forgive our impatience, perfect our faith
> and while we await the fulfilment of your promises,
> grant to us a good hope because of your word;
> through Jesus Christ our Lord, Amen.
>
> *Alternative Service Book 1980*

Who are these, like stars appearing,
  these before God's throne who stand?
Each a golden crown is wearing;
  who are all this glorious band?
    Alleluya, hark! they sing,
    praising loud their heavenly king.

Who are these of dazzling brightness,
  these in God's own truth arrayed,
clad in robes of purest whiteness,
  robes whose lustre ne'er shall fade,
    ne'er be touched by time's rude hand –
    whence comes all this glorious band?

These are they who have contended
  for their Saviour's honour long,
wrestling on till life was ended,
  following not the sinful throng;
    these, who well the fight sustained,
    triumph through the Lamb have gained.

These are they whose hearts were riven,
  sore with woe and anguish tried,
who in prayer full oft have striven
  with the God they glorified;
    now, their painful conflict o'er,
    God has bid them weep no more.

These like priests have watched and waited,
  offering up to Christ their will,
soul and body consecrated,
  day and night to serve him still:
    now, in God's most holy place
    blest they stand before his face.
        H. T. Schenck, 1656–1727, tr. Frances E. Cox

We preach not one advent only of Christ, but a second
also, far more glorious than the former. For the former

gave a view of his patience; but the latter brings with it the crown of a divine kingdom. For all things, for the most part, are twofold in our Lord Jesus Christ: a twofold generation; one, of God, before the ages; and one, of a Virgin, at the close of the ages: his descents twofold; one, the unobserved, like rain on a fleece; and a second his open coming, which is to be. In his former advent, he was wrapped in swaddling clothes in the manger; in his second, he covereth himself with light as with a garment. In his first coming, he endured the Cross, despising shame; in his second, he comes attended by a host of angels, receiving glory. We rest not then upon his first advent only, but look also for his second. And as at his first coming we said, Blessed is fire that cometh in the Name of the Lord, so will we repeat the same at his second coming; that when with angels we meet our Master, we may worship him and say, Blessed is he that cometh in the Name of the Lord. The Saviour comes, not to be judged again, but to judge them who judged him; he who before held his peace when judged, shall remind the transgressors who did those daring deeds at the Cross, and shall say, These things hast thou done, and I kept silence. Then, he came because of a divine dispensation, teaching us with persuasion; but this time they will of necessity have him for their King, even though they wish it not. (Cyril of Jerusalem, 315–86, *Catechetical Lectures*, 15)

Exercise
Read the Sunday paper with special care. Let it be a prompt for your prayer. What does it tell you about the hopes and cares of our world? What are your own personal hopes and concerns? How can the Gospel become a star for your inner being?

Monday 3 January 2000:
Renewal of Our Faith

'Everyone who calls on the name of the Lord shall be saved.' (Rom 10:13)

Faith empowers and strengthens us. Our own life of faith is not a personal possession. It is a gift of God, given to us and to our world.

Scriptural Reading

But the righteousness that comes from faith says, 'Do not say in your heart, "Who will ascend into heaven?" ' (that is, to bring Christ down) 'or "Who will descend into the abyss?" ' (that is, to bring Christ up from the dead). But what does it say? 'The word is near you, on your lips and in your heart' (that is, the word of faith that we proclaim); because if you confess with your lips that Jesus is Lord and believe in your heart that God raised him from the dead, you will be saved. For one believes with the heart and so is justified, and one confesses with the mouth and so is saved. The scripture says, 'No one who believes in him will be put to shame.' For there is no distinction between Jew and Greek; the same Lord is Lord of all and is generous to all who call on him. For, 'Everyone who calls on the name of the Lord shall be saved.' (Rom. 10:6–13)

Reflection

The communion which we have received through taking part in the celebration of Advent, Christmas and the New Year renews our innermost faith. We are reminded that everyone who calls

148

on the name of the Lord will be saved. No one is excluded from the saving purpose of God. It is not some kind of lottery, with winners and losers. The heart of God is big enough for all of us. That is why we do not have to earn the attention of God. It is given more generously than we can realise or know.

Our reading from Paul's Letter to the Romans is a powerful reminder that the earliest of the creeds or acts of faith was to acknowledge that 'Jesus is Lord'. To say that was to enter into the mysteries of salvation, to open our hearts to confess that God has redeemed us and we are justified. That is why it is safe to profess faith and to seek a renewal of faith so as to face the new century peacefully and with inner calm.

True faith enables us to let go. It allows us to relax securely back into a relationship of trust with God because we know that we are safe and saved. Like the Magi and all those who are truly wise, we follow the star to its logical conclusion, the place where the Saviour of the world waits to be recognised.

Prayers

Almighty and eternal God,
you have revealed yourself as Father, Son and Holy Spirit,
and live and reign in the perfect unity of love.
Hold us firm in this faith,
that we may know you in all your ways
and evermore rejoice in your eternal glory,
who are three Persons in one God,
now and for ever. Amen.

Collect for Trinity Sunday, *Alternative Service Book 1980*

All hail the power of Jesu's name;
let angels prostrate fall;
bring forth the royal diadem
to crown him Lord of all.

Crown him, ye morning stars of light,
who fixed this floating ball;

now hail the strength of Israel's might,
  and crown him Lord of all.

Crown him, ye martyrs of your God,
  who from his altar call;
praise him whose way of pain ye trod,
  and crown him Lord of all.

Ye seed of Israel's chosen race,
  ye ransomed of the fall,
hail him who saves you by his grace,
  and crown him Lord of all.

Hail him, ye heirs of David's line,
  whom David Lord did call;
the God incarnate, man divine,
  and crown him Lord of all.

Sinners, whose love can ne'er forget
  the wormwood and the gall,
go spread your trophies at his feet,
  and crown him Lord of all.

Let every tribe and every tongue
  to him their hearts enthral,
lift high the universal song
  and crown him Lord of all.

William Shrubsole, 1760–1806

I believe in one God, the Father Almighty, Maker of heaven and earth, and of all things visible and invisible.

And in one Lord Jesus Christ, the only-begotten Son of God, begotten of the Father before all worlds; God of God, Light of Light, very God of very God; begotten, not made, being of one substance with the Father, by whom all things were made.

Who, for us and for our salvation, came down from heaven, and was incarnate by the Holy Spirit of the

Virgin Mary, and was made man; and was crucified also for us under Pontius Pilate; He suffered and was buried; and the third day He rose again, according to the Scriptures; and ascended into heaven, and sits on the right hand of the Father; and He shall come again, with glory, to judge the quick and the dead; whose kingdom shall have no end.

And I believe in the Holy Ghost, the Lord and Giver of Life; who proceeds from the Father and the Son; who with the Father and the Son together is worshipped and glorified; who spoke by the prophets.

And I believe in one holy catholic and apostolic Church. I acknowledge one baptism for the remission of sins; and I look for the resurrection of the dead, and the life of the world to come. Amen.

Nicene Creed

Exercise
Think about the ways in which your own faith has been renewed over the last five weeks. Thank God for enabling you to say 'Jesus is Lord'. Stand up; face north, south, east and west; say out loud, 'Jesus is Lord' in each direction; notice how you feel.

Tuesday 4 January 2000: Renewal of Our Charity

'If we love one another, God lives in us.' (1 John 4:12)

The new year comes with new demands on our time and energy. God renews us by calling us to love.

Scriptural Reading

Beloved, let us love one another, because love is from God; everyone who loves is born of God and knows God. Whoever does not love does not know God, for God is love. God's love was revealed among us in this way: God sent his only Son into the world so that we might live through him. In this is love, not that we loved God but that he loved us and sent his Son to be the atoning sacrifice for our sins. Beloved, since God loved us so much, we also ought to love one another. No one has ever seen God; if we love one another, God lives in us, and his love is perfected in us. (1 John 4:7–12)

Reflection

Faith and hope and charity come together in the communion of our relationships. We are to love others as God loves us. This is the only currency which is recognisable to the life of faith.

'If we love one another, God lives in us.' What is love? How can we recognise it? If it is worth anything at all, it needs to be grounded in truth. That is why it is not enough to say, 'I love you'. Our actions have to match our words. 'God's love was revealed among us,' John says, highlighting the fact that the incarnation was an act of love, rather than a pious promise. God's words are mediated to us through the action of the Word: Jesus came to us and walked among us. He was born in oblivion and died in shame. He taught a gospel of love by living a life of love, a life given to others.

What is the most precious relationship in your life? How do you show your love? How do you put it into deeds? Jesus's great deed is completed. Every time we are loving and generous to others, we enter more deeply into his offering of self back to the Father. Every time we are selfless, the Holy Spirit is able to speak directly to those whom we love. In this way the life of faith, hope and charity leads us to Bethlehem, to the wooden manger and to Jerusalem, to the wooden cross. Ultimately they are transformed; the empty womb becomes the empty tomb.

Prayers

Lord, you have taught us
that all our doings without love are nothing worth.
Send your Holy Spirit
and pour into our hearts that most excellent gift of love,
the true bond of peace and of all virtues,
without which whoever lives is counted dead before you.
Grant this for the sake of your only Son,
Jesus Christ our Lord, Amen.

Collect for Pentecost 7, *Alternative Service Book 1980*

Come down, O Love divine,
seek thou this soul of mine,
and visit it with thine own ardour glowing;
O Comforter, draw near,
within my heart appear,
and kindle it, thy holy flame bestowing.

O let it freely burn,
till earthly passions turn
to dust and ashes in its heat consuming;
and let thy glorious light
shine ever on my sight,
and clothe me round, the while my path illuming.

Let holy charity
mine outward vesture be,
and lowliness become mine inner clothing:
true lowliness of heart,
which takes the humbler part,
and o'er its own shortcomings weeps with loathing.

And so the yearning strong,
with which the soul will long,
shall far outpass the power of human telling;

for none can guess its grace,
till he become the place
wherein the Holy Spirit makes his dwelling.
                    Bianco da Siena, d. 1434, tr. R. F. Littledale

These three men follow the leading of the light above, and with steadfast gaze obeying the indications of the guiding splendour, are led to the recognition of the Truth by the brilliance of Grace, for they supposed that a king's birth was notified in a human sense, and that it must be sought in a royal city. Yet He who had taken a slave's form, and had come not to judge, but to be judged, chose Bethlehem for His nativity, Jerusalem for His passion. But Herod, hearing that a prince of the Jews was born, suspected a successor, and was in great terror: and to compass the death of the Author of Salvation, pledged himself to a false homage. How happy had he been, if he had imitated the wise men's faith, and turned to a pious use what he designed for deceit. What blind wickedness of foolish jealousy, to think thou canst overthrow the Divine plan by thy frenzy. The Lord of the world, who offers an eternal Kingdom, seeks not a temporal. Why dost thou attempt to change the unchangeable order of things ordained, and to forestall others in their crime? The death of Christ belongs not to thy time. The Gospel must be first set on foot, the Kingdom of God first preached, healings first given to the sick, wondrous acts first performed. Why dost thou wish thyself to have the blame of what will belong to another's work, and why without being able to effect thy wicked design, dost thou bring on thyself alone the charge of wishing the evil? Thou gainest nothing and carriest out nothing by this intriguing. He that was born voluntarily shall die of His own free will. The wise men, therefore, fulfil their desire, and come to the child, the Lord Jesus Christ, the same star going before them. They adore the Word in flesh, the Wisdom in infancy, the Power in weakness, the Lord of majesty in the reality of man: and by their gifts make open acknowledgement of what they believe in their hearts, that they may show forth the mystery of their faith and understanding. The incense they offer to God, the myrrh to Man, the gold to the King, consciously paying honour to the Divine and human nature in union: because while each substance had its own properties, there was no difference in the power of either. (Leo the Great, d. 461, *Sermon* 31)

Exercise
Your faith, hope and charity are gifts you can bring to God with all the fervour of the Magi as they present their gold, frankincense and myrrh. Look at the Christmas cards you have received this year. Choose your favourite and look at it carefully. What draws you to this card more than the others? How does it call you to love?

Wednesday 5 January 2000: The Star in Heaven

'I see him, but not now; I behold him, but not near – a star shall come out of Jacob, and a sceptre shall rise out of Israel.' (Num. 24:17)

As the Magi draw near to the manger and greet the new child, so we move forwards, renewed and strengthened by an experience of faithful prayer and discipleship as we have gazed into the dome of heaven.

Scriptural Reading

For we did not follow cleverly devised myths when we made known to you the power and coming of our Lord Jesus Christ, but we had been eyewitnesses of his majesty. For he received honour and glory from God the Father when that voice was conveyed to him by the Majestic Glory, saying, 'This is my Son, my Beloved, with whom I am well pleased.' We ourselves heard this voice come from heaven, while we were with him on the holy mountain.

So we have the prophetic message more fully confirmed. You will do well to be attentive to this as to a lamp shining in a dark place, until the day dawns and the morning star rises in your hearts. (2 Pet. 1:16–19)

Reflection

The day has dawned; the Morning Star has risen in our hearts and it has three meanings for us. It is first and foremost a person, Jesus our Messiah and Saviour, who was born, died and rose for us and now shines in the dome of heaven. Then it is a gospel, a proclamation, a banner headline which says that God loves us unconditionally and that we can turn to God in absolute confidence and hope. Finally, it is a vision, something which continues to draw us, just as the Magi were driven on in pursuit of the infinitely desirable, yet utterly unknown. We can journey forwards in the inner world, into undiscovered dreams and hopes, into a relationship with God which is beyond our control, yet which depends on a simple 'yes' from us, a commitment to let go and let God move in mysterious ways to transform us.

We can also journey forwards in the outer world, taking care to 'grow and become strong, filled with wisdom' (Luke 2:40), just as the boy Jesus did, so that 'the favour of God' may be upon us. This means taking risks, as the Magi did. It means letting go of some of our deepest and most tenderly held convictions. It means exposing our minds to new ideas, even

156

ones which stretch and trouble us. It means being deeply committed to reconciliation, so that we will journey out in the name of this goal, even if our journey takes us a long way away from home. It means new encounters and finding that things are, in T. S. Eliot's words, 'satisfactory'. It means the ultimate encounter with Jesus who comes as our judge and merciful friend, the one who waits for us, Jesus whose Spirit first placed the gift of faith in our hearts and called us out to roam under the dome of heaven, searching for a person, an experience and now a new vision to strengthen us for a new millennium.

Prayers

Almighty God,
The light of a new star in heaven
Heralded your saving love.
Let the light of your salvation dawn in our hearts
And keep them always open to your life-giving grace.
We make our prayer through Christ our Lord, Amen.

The Divine Office

As with gladness men of old
did the guiding star behold,
as with joy they hailed its light,
leading onward, beaming bright;
so, most gracious Lord, may we
evermore be led to thee.

As with joyful steps they sped,
Saviour, to thy lowly bed,
there to bend the knee before
thee whom heaven and earth adore;
so may we with willing feet
ever seek they mercy seat.

As they offered gifts most rare
at thy cradle rude and bare,
so may we with holy joy,

pure and free from sin's alloy,
all our costliest treasures bring,
Christ, to thee our heavenly king.

Holy Jesus, every day
keep us in the narrow way,
and, when earthly things are past,
bring our ransomed souls at last
where they need no star to guide,
where no clouds thy glory hide.

In the heavenly country bright
need they no created light;
thou its light, its joy, its crown,
thou its sun which goes not down;
there for ever may we sing
alleluias to our king.

William Chatterton Dix, 1837–98

The star that was seen in the east we consider to have been a new star, unlike any of the other well-known planetary bodies, either those in the firmament above or those among the lower orbs, but partaking of the nature of those celestial bodies which appear at times, such as comets, or those meteors which resemble beams of wood, or beards, or wine jars, or any of those other names by which the Greeks are accustomed to describe their varying appearances. And we establish our position in the following manner.

It has been observed that, on the occurrence of great events, and of mighty changes in terrestrial things, such stars are wont to appear, indicating either the removal of dynasties or the breaking out of wars, or the happening of such circumstances as may cause commotions upon the earth. But we have read in the *Treatise on Comets* by Chaeremon the Stoic, that on some occasions also, when good was to happen, comets made their appearance; and he gives an account of such instances. If, then, at the commencement of new dynasties, or on the occasion of other important events, there arises a comet so called, or any similar celestial body, why should it be a matter of wonder that at the birth of Him who was to introduce a new doctrine to the human race, and to make known His teaching not only to Jews, but also to Greeks, and to many of the barbarous nations besides, a star should have arisen? Now I would say, that with respect to comets there is no prophecy in circulation to the effect that such and such a comet was to arise in connection with a particular kingdom or a particular time; but with respect to the appearance of a star at the birth of Jesus there is a prophecy of Balaam recorded by Moses to this effect: 'There shall arise a star out of Jacob, and a man shall rise up out of Israel.' (Origen, 185–254, *Against Celsus*)

Exercise

Try to identify three truly wise people whom you have admired in your own life and who have been an inspiration for you as you have journeyed. In what particular ways did each of them inspire you? Think about the gold, frankincense and myrrh they shared with you. Then pray for them each by name and thank God for their leading of you.

Thursday 6 January 2000: The Magi Visit and Depart

'Happy are those whom you choose and bring near to live in your courts. By awesome deeds you answer us with deliverance, O God of our salvation; you are the hope of all the ends of the earth and of the farthest seas.' (Ps. 65:4–5)

Our search for a guiding star, our search to understand the meaning of the dome of heaven, our search for God, are met at the feast of the Epiphany. Jesus is born for our salvation.

Scriptural Reading

In the time of King Herod, after Jesus was born in Bethlehem of Judea, wise men from the East came to Jerusalem, asking, 'Where is the child who has been born king of the Jews? For we observed his star at its rising, and have come to pay him homage.' When King Herod heard this, he was frightened, and all Jerusalem with him; and calling together all the chief priests and scribes of the people, he inquired of them where the Messiah was to be born. They told him, 'In Bethlehem of Judea; for so it has been written by the prophet: "And you, Bethlehem, in the land of Judah, are by no means least among the rulers of Judah; for from you shall come a ruler who is to shepherd my people Israel." ' Then Herod secretly called for the wise men and learned from them the exact time when the star had appeared. Then he sent them to Bethlehem, saying, 'Go and search diligently for the child; and when you have found him, bring me word so that I may also go and pay him homage.' When they had heard the king, they set out; and there, ahead of them, went the star that they had seen at its rising, until it stopped over the place where the child was. When they saw that the star had stopped, they were overwhelmed with joy. On entering the house, they saw the child with Mary his mother; and they knelt down and paid him homage. Then, opening their treasure chests, they offered him gifts of gold, frankincense, and myrrh. (Matt. 2:1–12)

Reflection

This is a timeless story. Here richness and might and majesty are met and recognised by absolute outsiders. Wisdom is met by wisdom. For a brief moment we see the splendour of the incarnation revealed to us. It is as though a curtain were being drawn back in the dome of heaven and, momentarily, we greet the God who lies beyond the veil of our limited consciousness and perceiving.

The shepherds heard the angels sing, 'Glory to God in the highest'. At that moment too, the dome of heaven was rent and we had a glimpse of the absolute glory of God. God is disclosed to us in this child, this boy, this man, this life, this death, this resurrection, this return to the Father, this sending forth of the Holy Spirit of light and joy and hope into our hearts.

What can our reaction be? We slip our feet into the footprints of the Magi. We walk with them to the manger. We experience their shock and surprise as they find the epiphany that awaits them there. We offer our gifts with theirs.

Then we do the bravest thing of all. We turn back with them. We set our faces to the new task, the new life that awaits us, a future that is unknown and quite precarious possibly. A future which is in God's gift. Amen.

Prayers

Your nativity, O Christ our God, has shed the light of knowledge upon the world. Through it, those who had been star-worshippers learned through a star to worship you, O sun of Justice, and to recognise in you the One who rises and who comes from on high. O Lord, glory to you! (Troparion for the Feast of the Nativity, *Byzantine Daily Worship*)

Brightest and best of the sons of the morning,
  dawn on our darkness, and lend us thine aid;
star of the east, the horizon adorning,
  guide where our infant redeemer is laid.

Cold on his cradle the dew-drops are shining;
  low lies his head with the beasts of the stall;
angels adore him in slumber reclining,
  maker and monarch and saviour of all.

Say, shall we yield him, in costly devotion,
  odours of Edom, and offerings divine,
gems of the mountain, and pearls of the ocean,
  myrrh from the forest, or gold from the mine?

Vainly we offer each ample oblation,
  vainly with gifts would his favour secure:
richer by far is the heart's adoration,
  dearer to God are the prayers of the poor.

Brightest and best of the sons of the morning,
  dawn on our darkness, and lend us thine aid;
star of the east, the horizon adorning,
  guide where our infant redeemer is laid.

Reginald Heber, 1783–1826

Today the Magi, the truly wise, find weeping in a crib him whom they sought for shining in the stars. Today the truly wise revere clearly revealed in swaddling clothes him whom they had long patiently awaited unseen in the heavens.

Today the truly wise ponder in profound amazement over what they see there: heaven on earth, earth in heaven, humanity in God, God in humanity, and him whom the whole universe cannot contain, confined in a tiny body. And immediately upon seeing, they profess with mystical gifts that they believe and do not argue: they acknowledge God with frankincense, the King with gold, with myrrh the one destined to die.

So it is that the Gentile, who was last, has become first: for then the belief of the nations began from the faith of the Magi. (Peter Chrysologus, 400–450, *Sermon 160*)

> Eternal God,
> who by the shining of a star
> led the wise men to the worship of your Son:
> guide by his light the nations of the earth,
> that the whole world may behold your glory;
> through Jesus Christ our Lord, Amen.
> Collect for Epiphany, *Alternative Service Book 1980*

Exercise
Thank God that you have been drawn right into the heart of the Advent, Christmas and Epiphany celebrations this year and that you have beheld his glory. Ask yourself where your star is now. Keep following it. Put this book away carefully.

INDEX

Texts

My thanks to the Reverend Leslie Burnham who chose the Scripture readings which are used in this book and to Judith Longman, my editor at Hodder and Stoughton, for her generous help and interest.